LAURIE CRITCHLEY has worked as a radio and print journalist, and has produced documentaries for radio. She is currently employed as a commissioning editor with The Women's Press in London. She is the co-editor of *Something to Savour: Food for Thought from Women Writers* (The Women's Press, 1996) and *Feast! Women Write About Food* (The Women's Press, 1996), and edits The Women's Press young adult series, Livewire.

GW00716693

A GLIMPSE OF GREEN
women writing on gardens

Laurie Critchley, EDITOR

First published by The Women's Press Ltd, 1996
A member of the Namara Group
34 Great Sutton Street, London EC1V 0DX

British Library Cataloguing-in-Publication Data
A catalogue record for this book is available from the British Library

ISBN 0 7043 4506 4

Typeset in 11/13 pt Bembo by Intype
Printed and bound in Great Britian by
BPC Paperbacks Ltd

PERMISSIONS

The Women's Press would like to thank the following:

The Antique Collectors' Club, Woodbridge, for permission to reprint an extract from *Wood and Garden* by Gertrude Jekyll published by them in 1981.

The Bryansground Press for permission to reprint 'A Gentle Plea for Chaos' by Mirabel Osler from *By Pen and By Spade: An Anthology of Garden Writing from Hortus*, edited by David Wheeler, copyright © Hortus.

Germaine Greer, care of Aitken & Stone, for permission to reprint 'Self Defence' from *The Revolting Garden* by Rose Blight.

Clare Hastings for permission to reprint an extract from *Gardening Letters to My Daughter* by Anne Scott-James.

A M Heath & Co for permission to reprint an extract from 'A Flower-Arranging Summer' taken from *Plant Dreaming Deep* by May Sarton, copyright © May Sarton, 1968.

Susan Hill, care of Richard Scott Simon, for permission to

reprint an extract from *The Magic Apple Tree*, copyright ©
Susan Hill

Lyons and Burford Publishers for permission to reprint an
extract from 'Enter a Non-Gardener', taken from *My Garden
and I* by Olive Pitkin.

Drusilla Modjeska, care of Barbara Mobbs, for permission to
reprint an extract from *The Orchard*, copyright © Drusilla
Modjeska, 1994.

The Estate of Clare Leighton, care of David Leighton, for
permission to reprint an extract from 'October', taken from
Four Hedges: A Gardener's Chronicle by Clare Leighton.

Jill Parker for permission to reprint an extract from *The
Purest of Pleasures*.

Penguin UK for permission to reprint extracts from: *The
Alice B Toklas Cookbook* by Alice B Toklas (Michael Joseph,
1954), copyright © the Estate of Alice B Toklas, 1954; *The
Butterfly Gardener* by Miriam Rothschild and Clive Farrell
(Michael Joseph/Rainbird, 1983), *The Outdoor Butterfly Gardener* copyright © Lane Charitable Trust for Conservation
1983; and 'Woman's Place' from *Green Thoughts: A Writer in
the Garden* by Eleanor Perényi, copyright © Eleanor Perényi,
1981.

Random House UK Ltd for permission to reprint the
extracts 'Never Spray Against Greenfly' and 'The Soil' from
The Complete Old Wives' Lore for Gardeners by Maureen and
Bridget Boland published by The Bodley Head.

Reed Consumer Books for permission to reprint excerpts
from *Break of Day* and *My Mother's House and Sido* by Colette,

translated by Enid Mcleod, published by Secker and Warburg Ltd.

Seal Press for permission to reprint 'Garden' from *All the Powerful Invisible Things: A Sportswoman's Notebook* by Gretchen Legler.

Rosemary Verey and Katherine Lambert, care of the Felicity Brian Literary Agency, for permission to reprint 'The Crossing House Garden' by Margaret Fuller from *Secret Gardens: Revealed by Their Owners* edited by Rosemary Verey and Katherine Lambert.

Alice Walker for permission to reprint an extract from *In Search of Our Mothers' Gardens*, copyright © Alice Walker, 1983.

Every effort has been made to trace the original copyright holders, but in some instances this has not been possible. It is hoped that any such omission from this list will be excused.

CONTENTS

INTRODUCTION

Like many women I know, I am a compulsive (if somewhat erratic) gardener. My garden comprises two window-boxes kept filled to overflowing and over which I have long given up hope of imposing any symmetry or order. I weed, water, do battle with aphids, and occasionally add to the mosaic. Mainly, I marvel that two such tiny containers of soil support such abundant and absorbing landscapes.

My pleasure in these glimpses of green is perhaps a response to living in the inner city. As roof gardener, Clare Hastings, notes 'When you are a flat dweller, any area of outdoor space is a bonus'. But evidence would suggest that more space is often matched by a greater inclination to garden. In 'Enter a Non-Gardener', Olive Pitkin traces her transformation into a 'confirmed worker-on-the-land' with her move to the countryside.

The many reasons why gardening is so engaging find expression in much of the writing here, from the simple to the sophisticated. Jill Parker writes of the satisfaction to be gained from such apparently mundane tasks as pruning and weeding while Grenadian novelist, Jean Buffong, makes the point that 'half an hour with my rake and shears is worth five visits to the gym'.

There is satisfaction too in the fruits of one's labours. As Alice B Toklas recalls in 'The Gardens at Bilignin', 'there is nothing . . . as thrilling, as gathering the vegetables one has grown'. For Miriam Rothschild, pleasure lies in providing a well-stocked 'pub' for thirsty butterflies while for Germaine Greer – aka Rose Blight – little can match the rewards of self-defence which a well-planned, thorn-ridden urban garden brings.

Underpinning such personal triumphs is the sense of gardening as a vital expression of women's creativity. Perhaps nowhere is this more superbly explored than in Alice Walker's 'In Search of Our Mothers' Gardens' in which she recollects her mother's talent for self-expression through gardening. Emily Eldridge Saville's vivid remembrance of the garden of her youth is testament to the garden as a focus for some of our earliest imaginings and creative endeavours while Susan Hill continues to express that creativity by conjuring up the ideal flower garden of her mind's eye.

Whether women have an inherently different approach to creativity than men influences Mirabel Osler's 'A Gentle Plea for Chaos' in which she observes that 'men seem more obsessed with order in the garden than women'. And as Manju Kak in 'Sairam's Garden' reveals, enthusiasm rather than the rule book may in fact be the more successful approach. (Points of view much appreciated when viewing my lopsided window-boxes – although this is not to suggest that women lack a facility for precision as Gertrude Jekyll's comments 'On Colour' make clear.)

Perhaps what most clearly distinguishes women's creativity in the garden (as perhaps elsewhere) is an awareness and appreciation of the wider connections. In exploring the resonances gardening holds, much of the writing here is equally an exploration of the ways in which the simple act of gardening puts us in touch with ourselves and with others.

The garden may be, as in Gretchen Legler's experience, an avenue for realising future possibilities or serve, as in Latha Viswanathan's 'After the Rain', as a point of connection between our childhood and adult selves, bridging cultures and continents. In Clare Leighton's 'October', an awareness of the garden as a cyclical counterpoint to the passage of our own lives is a subtle but insistent theme. Through the garden, change is transformed from a disturbing dynamic into a reassurance that 'the rhythm of life never stops'.

For others, the garden embodies friendship and companionship. That it may also represent a legacy of creativity, handed down through generations of women, is a common motif throughout this anthology, not least in Colette's tribute to her mother, 'Sido'. For Drusilla Modjeska, the question of whether a garden may be considered a work of art fades in comparison to its centrality as a link between a diverse community of women and an expression of their individual and shared hopes, perspectives and understandings.

That the garden 'nourished by memory and desire' often mirrors the many influences in our lives leads to May Sarton's observation that 'gardens are as original as people'. In exploring the 'grand passion' that gardening may become – with its unique combination of immediate, visceral pleasures and deeper resonances – Sarton shares the ways in which, for her, gardening is essentially intertwined with writing.

Gardens and books may at first glance appear to be incomparable. If the written word can be seen as solid and immutable, the garden can symbolise all that is change. Yet, as the writing in *A Glimpse of Green* reveals, these two apparent opposites often share similar places in women's lives – both as a source and expression of connectedness and creativity. Perhaps it is not surprising then that the inimitable pleasures of the garden find such vivid and eloquent expression in the writing gathered here.

Laurie Critchley

A Pot Garden

CLARE HASTINGS

Dear M,

When you are a flat-dweller, any area of outdoor space is a major bonus. I first became inspired on a hot, sunny day walking to the postbox. I noticed a couple barbecueing on their balcony and, not to be outdone, I rushed to the local garage, purchased my own barbecue and charcoal and proceeded to gain access to a very small area of roof outside the bathroom. At first this was not easy and required some mountaineering skills. Friends were made to clamber into the bath and then squeeze through a gap in the window (the sash cord had broken), and once outside nobody dared to move owing to lack of safety harness and railings. Now it's all very chic. I've moved the bath, you can shimmy through french doors, cling to the barley-sugar twisted railings and peer at the privileged in the gardens below.

Roof gardening is one of life's great pleasures, and is not referred to as container gardening for nothing. Everything is manageable, deadheading is a doddle, weeding non-existent, and you can re-organise colour schemes by shifting the pots around. The disadvantages are removing the débris, heaving bags of peat up several flights, ceaseless watering and, if you are very unlucky and misjudge the weight, house subsidence.

I was very fortunate when I started planning because I went

on a business trip to Spain. The unlucky van driver was commissioned on his homeward journey to stop off and fill the truck with terracotta pots. He took the task seriously, which was an excellent beginning. The English garden centres stock pots which are either cheap and dull or very pricey.

I wasn't creative at the start. Geraniums and fuchsias, the staples of the window-box, were potted everywhere. Now the whole effect is more haphazard and rambling. You *must* cram the pots. I try to fill every space, however small, with something. My pride and joy is the rose The New Dawn that is halfway up the wall now. I count the buds each week (you can do this with terrace gardening) and spray madly for greenfly. A clematis, C. Jackmanii, shares the same tub, along with some ivy and, this year, alyssum, pansies and violas. A lot of plants that are supposedly annual have managed to survive the frosts and are carrying on blooming, which is rather pleasing; my roof is obviously very sheltered.

Last year I grew sweet peas in a trough, which were a great success and looked very pretty twisted through the railings. I wish I had room to grow a row of beans or courgettes, perhaps I could just fit in another box – I rather fancy the idea of 'beans Finborough Road'.

I feed all the plants with liquid tomato fertiliser from time to time, water prodigiously each evening, otherwise you plan as the season goes along, transforming boxes in the time it takes you to go to the garden centre and back.

I do long to expand. Did you know that my main roof is flat? I am desperate to bang a hole up to it, and then I can start fully indulging my pot fantasies.

From **Gardening Letters to my Daughter,** *by Anne Scott-James, published by Michael Joseph.*

Garden

GRETCHEN LEGLER

Last week I staked my tomatoes. I pushed a tall, slim spike of wood into the soft ground beside each plant, and then, bending into the rich, acid greenness, I tied each thickest center stem up with soft rags, to hold each plant, to keep each plant from falling, so that the fruits grow high off the ground, where they can get sun.

Afterwards I washed my hands, and the smell and color of greenness came off of my fingers under the water with the soap. I could still smell tomato on my shirt sleeves, though, and it was still there on my fingertips when I put my hand to my nose, and I could see it under my fingernails and in the soft creases of my knuckles.

I thought then that I should give you something, now that you were leaving, moving on to a good job in another town, now that our work was done. Ours was a simple exchange and a clear one. I came to see you because I was miserable. It was your job to help miserable people. But I never expected a miracle to happen.

I thought, what I want to give you most is a ripe tomato, a tomato that grew from a plant that grew from a seed that I pushed into some soil, inside, in a small pot on the dining-room table in March, after I had first started talking to you. I had been telling you that I felt I needed to leave my husband but that I couldn't. I had ten thousand reasons, all breathlessly spinning out on top of one another. It was then that you asked me so plainly, 'What is it that you are most afraid of?'

I could give you a head of cabbage, purple or green, a stalk of broccoli, a yellow squash, a brown bag of shining cucumbers, a handful of hot red peppers, a bunch of basil, a long purple eggplant. All of these things I started from hardly anything, my back bent over tiny pots of black dirt, specks of seed in the deep palm of my hand, placing four seeds to a pot, one seed to a pot, covering them all with plastic in the end to keep them warm and wet until they sprouted. I planted them all in early spring, after I had first said to you, 'I'm afraid it isn't real. I'm afraid these are just *feelings*.'

I wanted to be with women, I told you. But maybe not. What did it feel like to want that? I didn't even know. Maybe I was making it up, all that wanting, all that heat in my body, all that desire, all that joy in the company of women, all of that crying and feeling like a stranger to myself. Maybe women weren't the issue at all. Maybe I had everything I needed right here with Craig. Maybe I just wanted trouble. Maybe I didn't know love when it looked me in the face.

What I really want to give you is some fruit from my garden, the ripest, most perfect, most delicious fruit. But it's not grown yet. It is all still small. It's been a cold summer. A good summer for lettuce and beet greens and herbs and snow peas. Not hot enough yet for the lettuce to bolt, but not hot enough yet, either, for the peppers to grow tall and blossom.

I love my garden. I love planting seeds. I love what I get back from it. For all I put in I get more back. For all the attention I pay it I am thanked over and over and over all winter long every time I sit down to eat. The garden makes simple demands. Water me. Weed me. Stake me up. Watch me grow. Then, harvest me when I'm ripe.

What I really want to give you is something that is a miracle, like a ripe tomato. What I really want to give you is a dense head of cabbage, started from a seed as small as the dot at the end of this sentence. A fair exchange for what you gave me. You said simply, 'Feelings are all any of us ever have, ever.' And this made immediate, startling sense. Feelings are real – desires, fears, joys. All of them. Real. They are what we have to go on.

When you start listening to the voices of your heart, they demand that you hear them all, and they have come to me all of a sudden now, asking me to attend to them. My own round, red, swollen heart has begun to talk to me. No, wait. This heart has been talking to me forever. It is only me now who has started to listen. This miracle I should keep for myself, you said. Then what have I for you?

Like I said, there are no tomatoes yet, no crook-necked yellow squash, no basil, no eggplants. They are still growing. By the time the first frost is two weeks away and you are long gone, I will be picking them by the boxful, making spaghetti sauce and pesto, making gazpacho and thick squash soup. I wish you could have some now. I wish I could give you some now, today, this minute, so you could hold one of my tomatoes in your hand, feel the weight of it in your palm.

From **All the Powerful Invisible Things: A Sportswoman's Notebook**, *published by Seal Press.*

A Letter from Mary Russell Mitford

to Emily Jephson

To MISS JEPHSON, Castle Martyr, Ireland
Three Mile Cross

18 May 1835

I write immediately, my dearest Emily, to say that we shall avail ourselves of the knowledge that plants can reach you safely, to send three or four pots with little geraniums (last year's cuttings), and the white chrysanthemum which you have not, and which the gardeners hereabouts call the button white. I hope that it will blow well. It is to other white chrysanthemums what the little Banksia rose is to other roses – only that the colour is as pure as milk, as lilies, as snow. I have not yet quite settled what geraniums to send; of course my best, but I am not quite sure which are my best. At present I meditate sending a 'Miss Mitford', or rather one of the 'Miss Mitfords', for there are several so called; it being a pretty proof of the way in which gardeners estimate my love of flowers, that they are constantly calling plants after me, and sending me one of the first cuttings as presents. There is a dahlia now selling at ten guineas a root under my name; I have not seen the flower, but have just had one sent me (a cutting), which will of course blow in the autumn.

I have your book of 'Irishmen and Irishwomen', dearest;

but I fear it would be dangerous to send that with the flowers. You must come and fetch it yourself. Yes, I know the beautiful tree peony, the lovely Indian-looking flower, so gorgeously oriental, and like the old rich Chinese paper which one sees in houses fitted up eighty years ago. What a size yours must have been! The camellias now-a-days and the rhododendrons and azaleas, and the hybrids between the rhododendrons and azaleas, are really wonderful; I have seen plants that have been sold for twenty guineas, and which to rich people are fairly worth the money. The most beautiful of either tribe that I ever saw is a large buff azalea of matchless elegance, still very rare. But, after all, I like geraniums better than anything; and it is lucky that I do, since they are comparatively easy to rear and manage, and do not lay one under any tremendous obligation to receive, for I never buy any. All my varieties (amounting to at least three hundred different sorts) have been either presents, or exchanges, or my own seedlings – chiefly exchanges; for when once one has a good collection, that becomes an easy mode of enlarging it; and it is one pleasant to all parties, for it is a very great pleasure to have a flower in a friend's garden. You, my own Emily, gave me my first plants of the potentilla, and very often as I look at them I think of you. You must send me some little seed in a letter, as a return for these plants, seeds of your own gathering and from your own garden; and it shall go hard but I will make them grow: any seed that you think pretty.

From the selected letters and recollections of Mary Russell Mitford as published in **My Garden**, *Sidgwick and Jackson.*

The Flower Garden

SUSAN HILL

I do not have a great deal to do with flowers in our garden. Vegetables and fruit are my province. I will spend any amount of time and energy on the growing of those. There is a streak of the puritan in me, which chides me that time spent on things which merely flower and possibly smell nice, are merely ornamental, is time frittered away. Nor will I do outdoor housework. There are suburban gardens which look as if someone has taken a vacuum cleaner and a duster to them every day. It also happens that there are rather a lot of flowers and shrubs I actively dislike. But, when summer does come, I always wish I had spent just a little more time the previous autumn and spring in planting and tending a lot of what I *do* like. I love sweet peas and always mean to dig and manure a trench for them, and make a tall support frame of twigs, at the same time as I am doing that for the runner beans and peas. Once you are embarked upon a job like that, it doesn't really take much more effort to double it up. But July comes and everyone else's sweet peas are a mile high and only then do I remember. So I rely on neighbours with a glut to give me some for the house. Sweet peas, like their edible cousins, will divide and multiply the more they are picked. They do not last very long indoors, but they smell sweet indeed and their sugar-almond pastels are so pretty.

I like to see flowers growing in the way old-fashioned

country gardeners always had them, in rows among the vegetables, with the sweet peas up behind the potatoes. Sweet williams grow wonderfully well like this, to be harvested with the carrots and the tiny spring turnips. If I were only allowed one flower in the garden I should be happy with sweet williams, for their spikiness and their clovey scent and their keeping qualities when picked – they will last a month in a vase if you crush the stems and change their water regularly. But sweet williams need to be started from seed in the autumn to flower the following year and I never get around to thinking about flowers in the autumn, so I end up by buying expensive plants in spring, just so as to have them, and with luck they may seed themselves, as wallflowers do, into perennials, albeit rather weakened and straggly.

There are a good many herbaceous border perennials I care for a lot, but whether from lack of nurture or dislike of our soil few will establish themselves and thrive here. A few spread all over, notably french marigolds and forget-me-nots and we have a good number of hollyhocks, pale pink and lemon and white and a deep blood-red. They are in all sorts of odd places and I only wish I could succeed with delphiniums in the same way, for I should love to have a great many of those very tall, very blue soldiers in the flowerbed outside the sitting-room window. They will not stay. Nor will aquilegia, those delicate, winged angels that look as if they are in flight. I have spent many a November hour putting in plants and they have died over the winter. So have ornamental poppies. But I shall try yet again this year, and every year until I succeed. One of the troubles, of course, is that we let the hens out into the garden, although never when there are seedlings about. But nothing can enjoy being so scratched around and loosened. Perhaps I shall give up any efforts to have a decent flowerbed. My heart is not really in it and the flowers know it. I shall go round Barley enjoying and envying other people their colours and scents and begging a few cut flowers where I can.

But there are one or two pipe dreams I have which may come true, if I make a serious effort. I long to see a lot of old roses flourish at Moon Cottage, all sorts of climbers, particularly scented, and to grow some lilies.

I have been warned off old roses by a lot of people. They are prone to every disease, I am told, temperamental and touchy, scarcely worth the trouble. That alone presents me with a challenge, but there is more to the matter than that. Old roses have character, and romance lingering in their pasts. They are like faded old beauties of Victorian and Edwardian country houses. I love their names and their rarity and the way they are ever so slightly blousy, and yet paper-frail, too. They have no resilience, come with no guarantees about their hardiness, or their eagerness to bloom non-stop from June to Christmas, if only you dead-head them. I shall have to restrict myself to varieties which do not mind being exposed, do not have to be pampered with a south-westerly aspect. I doubt if I shall ever be able to achieve the old rose garden I dream of so long as we are at Moon Cottage, but I shall make a start, in the bed near the boundary wall, which will give a little shelter, and perhaps, if things go well, in what is now my unsuccessful herbaceous bed, too. Old roses, alba roses, tea and damask and moss roses, most of them richly scented, many of them white or pink, which I prefer to reds and mauves. Belle de Crécy, Duchesse d'Angoulême, Félicité Parmentier, Madame Hardy, Wife of Bath, Mousse-line, Old Pink Moss, all of them will have a place and then, if I can find wall and fence space enough, I shall have the climbers, and three above all.

Albertine, of course. If there were only one rose in the

world I should want it to be Albertine, that glorious cascade of the pinkest pink. If I had a very high wall, I should like it tumbling over every inch of it. As it is, I have a small Albertine, growing over part of the low stone wall beyond the apple tree, where it has accommodated itself very happily. Up against the north wall of Moon Cottage, facing the Fen, I have begun to train a Gloire de Dijon, because it will tolerate the aspect. I should have liked to dare the incredibly beautiful Madame Alfred Carrière, and her cousin, Mrs Herbert Stevens, but there is not enough room for them to spread luxuriantly, or enough good rich soil below, in which to root them satisfactorily. If we removed the paving slabs all the way round the inner edge of the house, we could dig in manure and bone-meal and hope to have more climbers, primarily a scented honeysuckle. There is a cottage further up the lane whose whole front beneath its thatch is covered on one side with the rose Albertine and on the other with a sweetly-scented honeysuckle, and the two meet in the middle, to entwine and entangle in each other's arms over the front porch. To walk by on a warm June evening is to be transported.

The kitchen side of Moon Cottage, on the old wall that faces in towards the village, and is a little protected by the fence opposite and Mr Elder's cottage alongside, is covered with a very overgrown wisteria, which I do not greatly care for, and a deep purple small-flowered clematis, which I do. Getting rid of the wisteria will be a major operation, it is so well-established and rampant in all directions. Some of its foliage creeps and curls right in through the bedroom windows by June each year. There is a family dispute about it, for the others like the thing, but I plan to persuade them that they will like a pink, spring-flowering clematis, or a Mrs Herbert Stevens, even better.

Summer means sunflowers – better called by their exquisitely apposite French name, *tournesol*. It is folly to try and grow them very tall here, of course, the wild winds of the early autumn nights bend and break their thick stems and bow their great shaggy heads to the ground, but I do try never the less, because I love them so, their bright faces and open-golden look, and the way the bees swarm about them, I should like a whole marching line of them up against the wall near the woodshed. This year, we sowed two packets of seeds, and only a dozen plants came through. When they had reached what seems to be a vulnerable stage, a height of about six inches, half of these died, yet they are supposed to grow as easily as weeds. I have given them manure and peat, but perhaps they prefer not to be so richly fed. Next year, I shall leave them to seed themselves, and grow where they will.

The heads, when they go to seed, come into the house to be dried and then are hung out on a branch of the apple tree. A lot of birds come to feed off them and, if we are really lucky, there may be a goldfinch or two, a rare treat.

As soon as I have my conservatory, I shall make a serious attempt to grow some lilies, in pots, which is really the only way you *can* give them the exact soil conditions each particular variety likes best, and also the only way to move them about the place, according to the sun and shade. They look lovely in pots, too, though a really fine border thick with lilium candidum or regale is a sight to behold. I prefer those which are either pure white, or flushed through faintly with another colour, or tinged with it just at the heart – like Green Magic. They can be the most perfect flowers, but can also easily tip over that narrowest of dividing lines between splendour and absolute vulgarity. There are some hideous examples in the showier catalogues, violent orange and livid lemon, spotty or crudely streaked – as against delicately freckled.

One of the best things about lilies, of course, is their amazing scent. I shall put my pots of them under open windows, or beside an open door in the cool conservatory or the porch, leading from the front door, and be overpowered.

My mother thought lilies morbid funeral flowers, and could not bear to look at their stiff, waxy whiteness, nor smell what to her was the sweet stench of decay and death. Perhaps I find that hint of Victorian melancholy and funereal pomp in them attractive. If I had my fantasy garden, among the beds and beds of madonna lilies there would be a statue or two, of a winged angel, madly grieving.

From **The Magic Apple Tree: A Country Year**, *published by Penguin.*

New Color Schemes in the Garden

LOUISE BEEBE WILDER

Gardeners have become color conscious only in fairly recent years. Our grandmothers and great-grandmothers disposed their plants about their beds and borders with happy indifference to the din set up by warring hues in juxtaposition. Magenta and scarlet, rose and yellow mingled as unashamedly as in Czech embroideries. In formal regions the Victorians supplied some need in their consciousness by the use of crude contrasts; the scarlet of Geranium, the blue of Lobelia, the yellow of Calceolaria, often bound about by a hem of Dusty Miller, were repeated over and over from every parterre and park, and even quite small gardens affected this uncompromising quartette. It was Mr William Robinson, Dean of English gardeners, and Miss Gertrude Jekyll, who freed us from this strongly entrenched tradition. Mr Robinson showed us the folly of abject formality and turned our attention once more toward an appreciation of hardy plants used in a more or less natural setting. Miss Jekyll made us believe ourselves artists in embryo with a color box to our hands and a canvas ready stretched before us. She opened up to us a new delight in gardening and new possibilities in ourselves and set us a most radiant and enticing example.

But as so often happens the pendulum in its back swing went further than those who supplied its initial impetus intended. We found ourselves in the throes of such meticulous colour scheming that gardens though painstakingly harmonious in their color arrangements were almost as artificial in effect as in the old bedding-out days. This was particularly the fact in England where the color-schemers reached a high degree of proficiency. We Americans, for want of exact knowledge of our materials and the cantankerousness of our climatic conditions, rather lagged behind in this respect, but we did the best we could. Nice-minded ladies shuddered at the sight of a scarlet Oriental Poppy and the mere word magenta was enough to cause goose flesh to rise upon anyone who was anyone at all. All strong color was banished from polite purlieus – though it kept up a low muttering in the outlands – and we became chaste and chastened in our color predilections. Fragile mauves and buffs, shadowy blues, soft pinks and salmons, lavenders, heliotropes and saffrons, with an admixture of fleecy white flowers and gray foliage, were the only hues suffered in our garden.

And it must be confessed that the effects thus obtained were charming, gracious. But were they not a thought unsatisfying, a trifle weak in the last analysis? Did the eye not now and again become restless and cast about in search of a flash of scarlet, a glint of honest yellow?

In any case the pendulum has again begun to swing, propelled doubtless by a perhaps unconscious need for greater strength and vitality, more warmth and glow. Less aloof refinement in our gardens. The world is full of color to-day as perhaps never before. Artists splash it recklessly upon their canvasses, workers in applied design use it lavishly. Pottery, glass, fabrics, woods, embroideries, all show brilliant hues and bold associations of crude hues. We are color thirsty and may be in danger of becoming a little drunk with our new liberty – but gardens I think are going to be distinctly the gainers. We shall have contrast as well as harmony, richness and depth and brilliance as well as delicacy and refinement, and all used with a light touch and a freedom from rule of thumb that should make our gardens far more livable and interesting than they have ever been before.

One of the manifestations of this new color freedom is that magenta is no longer hall-marked as vulgarity, but has arisen from its Victorian grave and is invading the realms of draperies and women's belongings, thinly camouflaged by such titles as Fuchsia and Amaranth. Into gardens too it is boldly making its way worn by the fine new varieties of Rhododendrons, Primulas, Michaelmas Daisies, herbaceous Spiraeas, Pyrethrums and other flowers, and no one is pointing the finger of scorn at them. As a matter of fact pure magenta, especially when combined with a velvety texture, is one of the most lovely of hues and shows itself friendly enough in association with other hues provided the reds and salmon pinks – its inalienable enemies – are kept at a proper distance. With cream (Galtonia), with the low-toned corn-yellows (Digitalis ambigua), with the deep maroons such as are found among the Sweet Williams, with the lavender and silver of Catmint, with the cool blues (Campanula), with some shades of pure purple it is not only admissible but highly effective. Try Phlox Le Mahdi with pale yellow Gladioli, or Loosestrife with the tall, creamy Mullein, Miss Willmott. The old Mullein Pink (Agrostemma) is lovely with Nepeta and some of the new rich-toned Sidalceas are fine enough with the cold blue and silver of Eryngiums. One could multiply examples indefinitely.

Of course in gardens or at seasons where the reds and scarlets are to play an important part magenta must be reduced to a minimum, though it need not be wholly excluded. As elsewhere, color harmony in the garden is far more dependent upon the proportion of the color areas than the actual colors employed. To realize this fully we have only to turn to certain flowers; in certain Fuchsias we find magenta and scarlet, in a scarlet Cactus flower we find a magenta suffusion, in most of the wild Geraniums it is the fine magenta veining that gives the flowers their character and distinction; and it is the dark red calyx of the Cardinal flower that gives this brilliant wildling its rich effect. And so in the garden a patch here and there of some apparently discordant hue may tune the whole theme to a richer melody.

Personally I am delighted that the more vibrant hues are again to light our gardens – red, scarlet, orange, purple. I have had a bit of border at the back of my garden this summer that has given me much pleasure. It is primarily a red and white border but there are here and there a bit of pale pink, a little cool blue and some light yellow to take the edge – or the curse, if you like – off the brilliance. It began in May with the Tulips, Halley (Chinese red) and Colonel Cuney, a warmer hue, and several creamy and lemon-colored sorts, and progressed to masses of Sweet William Scarlet Beauty, a superb color, white Peonies, a pink Peony or two, pinky-scarlet *Lychnis Arkwrighti*, tall white and pale yellow *Aquilegia chrysantha* and a yellow Potentilla whose name I do not know. Now as I write it is bright with red and white Hollyhocks, dark red and salmon-colored Zinnias, Snapdragons, Dimorphotheca, and so on, the whole very gay and refreshing to look upon.

From **Adventures in a Suburban Garden**, *published by Macmillan.*

The Essence of Romance

EMILY ELDRIDGE SAVILLE

Once upon a time, before the days of motor cars and airplanes and radios and world-wars, there was a garden, and a day in June when it was full of roses; great sweet hundred-leaf roses, dark-red crisp glorious George the Fourth roses, beautiful yellow-centred single roses, sunshiny prickly yellow roses, tiny Scotch baby roses, ragged sweet Cinnamon roses, and pure white Baltimore Belles. The borders were glowing with their color, and the air was full of their sweetness. Somewhere overhead an oriole was carolling his bravest as the sun shone down on him and the roses and me — a little girl in a brown shady hat, living with Grandpapa and Grandmamma and Aunty Nan.

It was a wonderful place, that garden, up three steps from the square green yard. That was cool and quiet and shady from the elm branches overhead, and cut off from the street by a tangle of lilacs and syringas and such things. Under their foliage was a cool dark world with hard dry earth underneath, little crackly twigs all around and a fluttering greeny canopy overhead; with golden sunlight flickering through. One could be quite hidden there, play all alone and quite safe from highwaymen or smugglers or cows and things if ever they came; but the garden was full of color and sunshine and fragrance and the happy hum of bees.

I loved the garden, and I always spelt it in my diary with

a capital G. It told me things. In the midst of a forest of asparagus plumes, under the luxuriant shade of the trumpet vine, sitting carefully down – cross-legged – in the midst of riotous bloom I could see and smell and listen and make-believe. There were many paths, very trim and orderly, and every path had box borders and a different interest at the end. There were big square tulip beds riotous with color in their day, and there were borders full of myrtle and grape hyacinths and lilies-of-the-valley and violets. Under the archway in the grape trellis was a long path leading to the left past the herb garden with its border of larkspur and monks-hood to the stone seat under the pear tree, all fragrant with lemon balm. To the right it ran past the two old box trees 'Baucis and Philemon' to the vine-covered wall, where, climbing to the top, I would watch the carriages toiling up the hill. The box trees were very old, and one of them had a hole in the middle quite large enough for a play-house for a little girl if someone would lift her in; and all along there were phlox and peonies and day-lilies and Sweet Williams and everything else in its time. I loved the peonies, they were so brave! On to the great trumpet vine archway, to the left the path led past the vegetable house to the summer house with its hammock and its shade and its honey-suckle vines. The vegetable house was a joy and a mystery. It was nearly buried in the ground, with a rounded roof like an Igloo Hut or an old Cornish Church, and entirely smothered in flowering vines.

To the right was a leafy bower of flickery light and shade where I played dolls through the fence with Jessie Mills. Katy Ragan always said that Jessie Mills was too big to play with the likes of me. Grandmamma had said that there would not be such a difference in our ages by and by. I wondered why? She could wear any dress she liked and she had a bracelet, and she sat up until nine, but she was not too big to wriggle through the fence one day, and we walked up and down arm and arm very lovingly. 'This' — I told her — 'I call Saint James's path because of Grandpapa, and this Saint Anne's because of Grandmamma, and this' — the stone seat in the tangle of rosebushes overshadowed by the five fingers of an old pear tree — 'Grandmamma calls her "*Chapel of Ease.*"' Sometimes she reads here. She says the sun shines away the cobwebs and the birds make her glad.'

In a quiet corner of the Chapel of Ease were two secrets all my own, one sad and one gay. One little garden bed was mine, and in the Spring under careful supervision I had planted my name, in mustard and cress, and it came up, embarrassingly plain; then I planted, all alone, two rows of orange and lemon seeds meaning to save out enough of the fruit for next winter and (laudable intention) give the rest away. At the same time I had planted a little slip of a wonderful flowering shrub given me by a little, great-great-Quaker Aunt, eighty-five years old. It would grow very quickly, she said, and its flowers would smell like pineapple. She knew, for she lived in a world of flowers — everything that came her way bloomed, they said, because she loved it so. Long after the mustard and cress were gone, I watched the little sprig and carefully pulled it up now and then to see if the roots were coming on and kissed it — and put it back again; but it died. Quite brown and stiff it grew, so I dug a safe deep hole, and laid it in, and patted it down, and put a little brown stone at the end, and waited every day for the little dove-colored Aunt to come trotting down the path and ask, 'Where is your little calycanthus, Elsie Ware?' I felt very guilty and quite sad until one day I found the oranges and lemons in two rows of vigorous shoots all shining green. But I never told Jessie Mills about them; they were all my own.

From **Memories and a Garden**, *self-published in 1924.*

Self-Defence

ROSE BLIGHT (AKA GERMAINE GREER)

If your garden is all that stands between your domestic hearth and a tourist-junkie-drunk-and-football-fan-infested street, you need to cultivate plants which actually inflict pain upon the unwary interloper. A large holly-bush will defend itself adequately against a toppling drunk or swooning dope-fiend, but, as it is very slow growing, it may be more rewarding to concentrate upon the more intractable roses.

Rosa felipes 'Kiftsgate' is able to strangle full-grown elms. The euphoric freak, about whom she throws her hammer-lock, will indeed die in aromatic pain. If he struggles to break free of her iron caress he may well flay himself to the bone.

The very existence of the 'Dunwich Rose' is justified by its astonishing ability to draw blood with its larger spines and to cause weeks of agony with its myriad tiny ones. *Rosa spinosissima* is so extravagantly prickly that it tears all its own leaves off in a high wind.

Most of the really vicious roses only flower as an after-thought, so that passers-by are not actively lured to donate blood and curses. The way to do that is to plant the showier hybrid roses on the far side of a killer rose. Passers-by will willingly run the gamut as soon as the buds begin to blow, and will abuse you roundly when they hurt themselves, all of which is very amusing, unless you loathe leathery hybrid roses and count the game not worth the candle.

Even more dreadful than the dreadful passer-by is the London dog. The combination of a dog and owner is a law unto itself, as I realised when I watched a dog-owner hold open my gate so that her deformed pooch could direct his steaming ammoniac jet right into the smiling faces of my auriculas.

The dog having his eyes and nose close to the ground is relatively vulnerable. *Berberis x stenophylla* has wonderful, long, hidden barbs at dogs' eye level. The handsome and useful spurge family is united in its habit of secreting corrosive latex if some fatuous quadruped should bruise its leaves.

From **The Revolting Garden**, *published by Private Eye/André Deutsch.*

CLARE LEIGHTON

Our potato crop waits to be dug. As I fork up a root and scrape a potato with my fingernail the skin slips off. All around us work shouts to be done. We have no time now for quiet enjoyment of our garden, for the first frosts and the autumn rains will soon be upon us, checking our digging and planting.

We enjoy digging our potatoes. It is the big treasure hunt of the year, even more exciting than searching for the fruit in the tangle of straw round the strawberry plants. The excitement lies in the anticipation we feel each time we stick the fork into the ground. How many potatoes will there be beneath this plant? This anticipation never tires, even after rows of digging. Here is all the mystery of an unknown, invisible harvest. We can see the extent of our peas and beans, and we know that each green-leafed parsnip top will have a corresponding root below, but who can tell how many potatoes huddle beneath the plant that we see above the ground? As my fork brings up the cool, moist potatoes, I lay them out in the sun to dry. They look beautiful as they lie on the earth in creamy rows. The limp, fading haulms curve away from them by their side in regular lines. Minute, undeveloped potatoes cling to the tendril roots of the plants, smooth of skin and fresh of colour in contrast with the decay of the aged seed potato. A robin sits near us on the haft of a spade and sings his autumn song to the worms that I unearth; they are many, and they wriggle back below the soil as fast as they can. But the robin is too quick for most of them, and he has a great feast. From time to time my fork spears a potato; in its damaged centre I find lovely small pink worms coiled tightly round.

Digging exposes an independent living world below the surface of the earth. Among the persisting roots of bindweed is the home of the burnt-coloured brittle wireworm; here it will live for nearly six years before it escapes above the soil as the click beetle. The little woodlouse wanders about, ready to coil itself into a ball at the slightest vibration. The centi-pede twists its body until it is the shape of a switchback at a fun-fair. Rubble and bits of broken crockery speak to us of men who knew this field before our day. But it is a world that flings us back in time and makes of the clods we turn pages of history, for one day among the marigolds we dug up a local money token of the eighteenth century. Relics of Roman Britain are scattered among our earth as broken pieces of brick; they are many, for we are on the edge of the Icknield Way, which was used as a Roman road. Our imagination one day was especially excited by the finding of the tooth of a wild board. Instantly our garden seemed full of perils, and civilisation shrank to a thin veneer of three inches of chalky soil. We have kept the tooth, and when life grows too respectable and secure, a glance at it reassures us with a thrill of fear.

But we grow bored with the endless surgical work in the garden. The summer's drought had checked the growth of the weeds, but now, after the September rains, they burst above the earth and cover the garden with enviable exuberance.

We have decided that the only inspiriting way to rid our

garden of weeds is to organise a campaign against special enemies. If we destroy certain weeds each year we may hope one day to have a clear garden. Unfortunately, we are surrounded on most sides by meadowland and unkempt gardens, so that dandelion seed and thistledown drift across our hedges in the wind and settle happily on our flower beds. It is a hard struggle. This year we have been waging war against groundsel and bindweed. Our fighting spirits have been so strongly roused that I have known us instinctively get off our bicycles in the country lanes to destroy a particularly big clump of groundsel. The groundsel is an easy enemy to vanquish, for its root comes out of the ground with ease, and one has no qualms about its destruction. But the bindweed is so lovely, with its flowers striped like the pink and white cotton frocks of young girls, that one is tempted to say that it is not a weed. It was only when our plants were nearly strangled by it that we became ruthless. Now we search the earth for the loose white strings of its roots, knowing that it is a wandering and tenacious creature.

There is some hope in weeding, for the weeds may one day be defeated, but the tidying of the garden is as exacting and unending as the daily washing of dishes. Soon the time of growth will stop for the winter, but still the lawns grow against the edges of the flower beds, and still the grass banks need regular clipping. . .

This is the time of year when everything drops into the earth. In spring there is an upward movement all around one, with a lift in plants and trees. Now it is the time of weight, when seed pod and berry, fruit and leaf fall and return to the earth. It is truly the Fall, a lovelier word for this season than autumn. The horse chestnut has cast down its shining fruit, warm of colour as it breaks from its tight-fitting, kid-lined case; on the soggy ground all round lie these lumpy, horned shells. The winds blow down pears, and we find them yellow and brown, surrounding the trees at their base. So we strip the fruit trees, our pleasure in picking tempered by the sight of the trees bare of colour for another year. It will be such fun when our young apple trees have grown tall enough to need ladders for the apple gathering. For this is an essential part of the ritual. I remember Aunt Sarah's trees in Berkshire when I was a child. They were old and gnarled and high, and I climbed ladders and strained and stretched to reach the topmost bough. Always the highest apple would shake away from me and stay there in defiance at the tip of the tree well into early winter, until one night of storm would blow it to the ground, where it would lie bruised and weather-worn, to be eaten by ants. But this will come with years.

As the garden gives up its fruit, so must we feed it, to renew its strength. Realist though I am, I find it hard to grow enthusiastic about the close-up smell of pig manure. One may pass a farmyard and enjoy the diffused smell of 'muck' that drifts out, but it is a different thing when the pile of manure is outside one's front door. The carter from the farm down in the plain has dumped our manure literally a few yards from the door. It is grand stuff, short and with very little straw; but that makes it smell even stronger. Noel and I set to work to move it... Fortunately, we grow more accustomed to the smell as we work, though, as we distribute it over all the garden there is no refuge in which we can escape it. The roses have bloomed this year in such abundance, and there has been so little nourishment in the dry soil, that we must be liberal as we feed the garden. We console ourselves for the unpleasantness of the work by telling each other that our gratitude to the flowers and trees is a poor thing if it shrinks from an unpleasant smell. As we cart barrow-loads of the food to different parts of the rose bed and the vegetable plots, I mind the smell less by recollecting the glamour that manure always holds for gardeners. I have never heard one of them mention the smell, except approvingly. I think they feel that the stronger the smell the better the stuff. Especially I remember our first gardener, Anderson. He used to lick his lips and his eyes would gleam and glow as he saw a load of steaming pig manure. 'That's good stuff,' he would purr. 'That's lovely, that's lovely. And don't it smell grandly ripe! Beautiful stuff!' With delight he would toss it down over all the beds, and dig it in round a tree, stamping on the bare manure in his exuberance. He was the true romantic. And so why should I allow an ecstasy to pass me by? It's grand stuff, this manure!

As we feed the garden, we review the damage done by the summer's drought. In persistent rain we look at the dead beech bushes that would have been saved by even a fraction of the wet we are having now. We count the gaps: four in the front, six at the back and one against the rubbish heap. Two or three cherry trees are half dead, but may just be saved. . .

How it rains these days. In the grass by the hedges, large shiny slugs appear, black as liquorice and beautiful of shape as they stretch themselves out. They heave like ships on a rough sea in their passage across the grasses. The garden is sodden and the trees drip, their autumn colours deepened and burnished by the wet. But roses and violas still bloom, and carnations are in bursting bud. Michaelmas daisies are untouched by frost and the cosmos still shows pink among its seeding heads. We can gather bowls of bright-coloured flowers for the house.

Into this sodden, dismal wet strike gleams of sun, with rainbows. In one day I see six. They link up hill with hill, bewitching the beechwoods that already turn colour for the Fall.

It is the month of the Hunter's Moon. We walk in the garden in moonlight. The rows of leeks and celery and parsnips assume a look of importance, mysterious in their masses of dark shade and silver flecks. The trees throw shadows across the ground, demonstrating the subtleties of their shape to us as they can never do in the daytime. Each small bush adds grandeur to its person. This silver light ennobles everything.

And then, on a dismal afternoon at the end of the month, I hear a particularly sweet bird song. Outside, in one of the flower beds, is a goldfinch on a cosmos plant. He has discovered that the cosmos is in seed. As I am enjoying the beauty of his red and black and gold, he flies off, leaving the flower-bed colourless and dull. I am turning from the window, disappointed at the shortness of his visit, when I hear a rush of wings and look out again at the flower-bed. The pioneer goldfinch has returned, bringing with him a 'charm' of the gaily coloured birds. They sing and twitter as they fly from plant to plant, pecking at the ripened seeds. I stand quite near them at the open window and they are unafraid. In their brilliant colours and their drooping flight they are like lighted Chinese lanterns swinging in a garden in a slight breeze. They have illumined for us a grey day.

In this time of decay in the garden the rhythm of life never stops. The chestnut tree throws off its leaves, exposing, where the leaf stem had been attached, that shapely mark of a horse-shoe, nails and all, that gives to the tree its name; but it is the swelling of next year's bud that pushes off the old leaf. Around the dead stalks of this year's lilies sprout green shoots of next year's plants. Growth has started in the fox-glove seedlings, and young cornflowers appear around the still-flowering plants. Autumn is not the sad time it is supposed to be. Darkness falls at five o'clock, and the garden is cold and wet, but it is a season of planning and expectation. It is now that we plant our bulbs, in itself an act of faith. How, then, can autumn be called dull and hopeless? Even the fallen leaf is food for future years of foliage and fruit, and promises next summer an added colour to the flowers.

From the chapter, 'October', in **Four Hedges: A Gardener's Chronicle,** *published by The Sumach Press.*

After the Rain

LATHA VISWANATHAN

Lightning sizzles near the window. A Louisiana thunderstorm is beginning outside. My dog rattles pitifully by my bed. I murmur soothing words, watch him pace the room diagonally for a long, restless minute before getting up. The monsoons of my childhood were always grand, full of drama. Clutching a mug of Darjeeling in my hand, I hurry to the patio door of my sunroom so I can enjoy a better view of my garden. In the half dark, thunder sends creatures scurrying into secret hiding places. Frogs rustle between clumps of monkey grass. A stripe of lightning and a corner comes to life, river oak branches reaching out. Tails of Spanish moss wave like Swami beards in the wind, taking me back.

Every June in Bombay, a net of fireworks was tossed into the sky. The rain came down in pellets, unrelenting, washing the earth of scorching heat, heaving gutters, turning roads into ribbons of coffee-coloured sea. Sometimes, late in the afternoon, a brief respite. The soil gleamed as though sequins had fallen from the sky. Earthworms crawled everywhere, wriggling designs at the foot of the banyan tree I passed. My classmates, so dainty, oohed and stepped aside. One of the boys split the worms in two with his feet, watching them multiply. As I walked home, I sneaked a look at a family on the pavement, tarpaulin tent for a roof, huddled inside. I was glad of my home, Amma waiting with hot Ovaltine.

Away from the city for the long holidays in the summer-time, I roamed the garden of my grandparents, smack in the middle of a tiny village, close to the southern coastal countryside. Here I learned to moisten banana stem strings in water, casting on with deft fingers, knotting together lotus petals, roses, jasmine, oleanders and chrysanthemums – stands for the gods. I saved the ends for my braids, hugging the fragrance close to my face. While grandmother circumambu-lated the holy *tulasi*, the sweet-basil plant that occupied centre stage in the backyard, I discovered that juice from its crushed leaves soothed the itch of rashes, ant and mosquito bites that covered my arms.

When the maid came to the house in the mornings, the garden well became the focus, water vessel gurgling hour after hour. I ran to help her often, loving the music of plop and splash, the accompanying wheel screeching on top.

After the rain, I complained about earthworms every-where, shimmying all around. 'A gardener's ally,' grand-mother said, 'like the praying mantis over there.' Earthworms, I learned, were quite headless and very deaf. Dancing at my touch, they gobbled up soil, excreting it in a different form. I wondered if their equanimity came from combining the physical best – manly this end, feminine the other. They tunnelled tirelessly as I watched. How I admired the civic sense of their plan, working to enhance air quality for the community, visible and invisible creatures all.

In the centre of my American garden, there is a fountain-cum-bird-bath. Dotted around it are shrubs, trees that burst with bright flowers at different times. Lotus-coloured azaleas, crepe myrtle in silk magenta, waxy magnolias and gardenias. My braids are gone, my hair is thin and lightly streaked with gray. Yet I cannot resist plucking an oleander and tucking it into my hair. Yesterday, when I handed my daughter one, 'What do I do with it?' she asked. Her hair is too short.

The storm abates. I hear the geckos calling, tree frogs singing, spot a visiting egret from the swamp behind. Cardinals the colour of hibiscus step gingerly into my fountain. My daughter calls for me. Born in temperate Canada, 'What's all that strange noise?' she says. I climb into bed with her. The sounds get fainter here like echoes of the past. On her desk, in a bowl from craft class, an oleander sits – her miniature garden, a *tokoniwa*.

Later in the morning, as the sun comes up, chameleons dart everywhere, neck balloons puffing out. Monty, my German Shepherd dog, grins and cracks puddles. He chases a baby snapping turtle, a visitor from a creek nearby. The Cyprus tree that collapsed during Hurricane Andrew is now a stump, covered with fire ants. If the soil were redder and the mound two feet bigger, it could be a snake pit in an Indian village. Pulling dry foliage from my yucca plant, I peek into the middle without thinking. Tadpoles in bromeliad navels, as real today as they were in the past. I see my cousins and myself squatting in the grass in cotton petticoats, eating whole mangoes while the crows watched.

My daughter has friends over. They suck orange popsickles and make mudpies. Cousins are far away, mangoes come in bottles and cans.

For me, the garden is a place where things are simple, the two of us developing side by side. The world does not intrude here, judgements, egos are cast aside. Time zigzags, I am here and there, child and adult, guru and disciple at the same time. I may be by myself, but I am never alone. There is a whole community at my feet. The garden helps me to renew myself, scale down, evaluate what is truly important in life. The earthworm, that lowly life, teaches resilience. Life changes, it says, whether I submit or not. Here all creatures are truly equal, the scale is so large.

When I see the damp surface of my garden writhe with the familiar shapes, I stop weeding and wipe the sticky juice of bruised stems from my palms. I bend down and take a moving clot of soil in my hand. It never ceases to amaze me, this persistent ability of the earth, the purposeful activity that goes on whether or not I am around. A garden should not be fully under my control, I realise, the earth has her own infallible plan. Soil scientists tracing the spread of earthworms uncovered that many of the hard-working species are not native to America. These silent underground inhabitants work endlessly, offering precious nitrogen through droppings – ammonia, urea and uric acid – elements that naturally enhance the quality of the topsoil, creating a hospitable base for the growth of more plants. These burrowers, immigrants like myself, they tell the truth. This place I call mine with such pride, why I'm only a transient here, a visitor for a while.

Inside the house, the kitchen is cool, dipped in green from the magnolia tree outside. There's *rasam*, spicy soup simmering on the stove, the way grandmother made it, with tomatoes from the garden. Through the window, I see my Cajun neighbour, eighty-eight years old and fiercely inde-pendent, trudging towards the mailbox. She stops to yank a dandelion in the middle of the lawn. When she smiles and waves, she reminds me of my grandmother. Sparrows chatter high up in the pyracantha tree, scattering red berries like almonds, taking off in a huff.

If the day is rough, words tumbling out all wrong; when images of perfection pound at my temples, I seek the earthworms, my garden, this earthly balm. After the rain, spirit unleashed by the storm, it willingly, efficiently, cleans my head.

The Soil

BRIDGET BOLAND

I hate the use of the word 'soiled' to mean indiscriminately 'dirty'. Soil is clean and it is beautiful, and hands (and boots, too) covered with it are only as they should be. I love to get my hands in the earth on a warm day and feel how live it is – as live as any flower or animal, it almost pulses. I love to feed it, and my conscience, which sometimes stops me buying plants I want, can never get a word in edgeways when it is a question of buying manure.

People say poultry manure is too hot, because they can't be bothered to treasure it long enough – keep it for two years, in a heap with alternate layers of wood-ash, and there is nothing better.

A compost heap is also a lovesome thing. In our twenty feet by twenty feet garden in London (where I had a very small heap and was forever poking among it in search of the 'red flat-tailed lobworms' which the books said it should produce, and my worms never seemed particularly red and their tails were sort of pointed), it appeared to me that potato peelings took far longer to rot than the rest, and even to slow down the whole heap. I took to keeping them separately in a wooden crate alongside, where they rotted splendidly in no time. I found that delicious goo oozed out between the slats, so I kept a tray under part of it that could be slid out like a drawer, and, diluted with as much water, made a fine

40

liquid fertiliser. The hessian bags that some plants come in from nurseries, filled with a little animal manure from your heap and kept in a bucket of water by it, make a lovely liquid manure, too.

A correspondent told me how, in her childhood in Scotland, the family used to complain that her mother lavished more food than she ever gave her offspring on the marrow she was growing for a prize, in fierce competition with the episcopalian vicar of a neighbouring parish, and that the vicar, with the aid of prayer, was in a stronger position than she was anyway. Her mother won the prize, and remarked: 'Prayer is all very well, but there's nothing to beat the best minced steak.'

A more sinister story was told me about another vicar, who could never be induced to part with the secret of how he grew such fabulous roses, until finally some ladies of the parish cornered him and bullied it out of him: 'I bury a cat under each bush,' he said.

From **The Complete Old Wives' Lore for Gardens,** *published by The Bodley Head.*

I Heard the Shears Call My Name

JEAN BUFFONG

Looking out of my bedroom window into my snake-shaped garden, I see my rose bushes standing like bodyguards over the frost-bitten shrubs. Tiny green shoots of new daffodils push gently but defiantly through the frozen earth to gulp new air. Even in its neglected state, my garden is a paradise compared to when I first moved in. At that time, the only trespasser was a single rose bush, its branches twisted around the boundary fence and covered in a thousand tiny pink flowers. It was one of the things that helped me make up my mind about moving in. The garden with its single blooming bush represented a kind of hope, something to nurture and cherish. The garden itself a place of escape from the rat race of life.

As a child back in the Caribbean, I was forever sowing and planting. The front of my home was my main canvas. As it was paved with no earth to dig, I used empty tins of different shapes and sizes to make my garden. Pink, white and red jump-up-and-kiss-me, red-and-white batchelor buttons, multi-coloured lady's-slippers and red dangling cats'-tails formed a border to the front door. Under my window, a single buttercup grew where I had found a crack in the concrete. From different angles, my garden looked like a strip of patchwork quilt. From the sky – according to my imagination – an earth-bound rainbow.

42

I would reposition my tins to create different landscapes and patterns. This would often involve consulting the plants themselves, including asking the pink-and-white daisies in the short milk tin if they'd like to keep company with the lilac batchelor buttons. I thought at the time that the batchelor buttons needed a new girlfriend. Lifting the daisies, I knocked over a pail of crotons. 'Croton,' I snapped at the flowers splashed on the ground, 'What's the matter with you, child? You don't have to be so jealous of daisy.' I was so engrossed, I did not hear my aunt Clarita come into the yard. As I recall, she gave me a good telling off for pretending that flowers were people – and 'big people' at that. It didn't stop me – my mother knew of my flower friends.

Today, I still find my escape route from reality among my plants – not in the sun-baked Caribbean but in wintry Walthamstow. I have exchanged my tins of jump-up-and-kiss-me and batchelor buttons for daffodils, tulips, fuchsia and sweet williams. My flower tins have replaced by a wire-fenced garden an acrobat's leg-split in width. Here, after a stress-packed day, I unwind, conflicts fusing into the earth. Half an hour with my rake and shears is worth five visits to the gym.

After a particularly gruelling day at work, even my habitual cup of tea takes second place to the garden. Bag down, coat off, I pick up my garden shears and rake, and head straight outside. I may pour out all the day's problems to the rose bush that still clings to the boundary fence – and exchange a few words with the geranium in the corner by the small shed. Weeding – usually a superb outlet – is now off-limits after an occasion last summer when, charged with irritation, I set out to weed the garden and swept up all the new seedlings in my rage. These days, I stick to cleaning up the lawn.

Click, click, clickety, click. I introduce the shears to the grass. Click, click, clickety, click. Off with the heads of the wandering dandelion. Click, click, clickety click. With each blade of grass, a degree of the day's baggage slides from my shoulders into the ground. Click, click, clickety, click. My body and heartbeat begin to move to the rhythm of the shears. It takes about seven minutes to lose myself completely – which I do. After a particularly rough day last summer, I even thought I heard the shears call my name.

'Jean . . . Jean!'

Unfortunately, the voice was Sally's – my back-to-back neighbour.

I ignore her.

'Jean,' she calls again. 'I heard the shears and knew it could only be you. Do you want to borrow my lawn mower? It must be hard on your back.'

Click, click, clickety, click. My hands move faster and faster – so quickly in fact that they stray and clip off the stem of my favourite white lily. Click, click, clickety, click. Go away! I think.

'Hey, Jean!' This time, it's the more welcome voice of my neighbour on the left.

'Hi, George.' Click, click, clickety, click.

'Who or what provoked you today? You're attacking the grass like it's somebody's neck you're after.'

Before I can answer, Sally informs George that she's offered me the use of her lawnmower because bending down will surely give me back pain.

'Mower!' laughs George. 'Jean don't want a mower. She can't dance with a lawnmower.'

I straighten my back. 'Shhh! Don't let out my secret, George,' I laugh.

'What *are* you two on about?' Sally wants to know.

'Sally, don't tell me that in all these years of Jean living here you haven't noticed her dancing in the garden. Doing the shoe shuffle with the shears and the quick step with the rake.'

The expression on Sally's face sends me into a fit of laughter.

And although George is teasing me, what he's said is true. I not only sing in tune with the shears and step in time, I'll also occasionally quick step while raking up the grass. Click, click, clickety click. Quick, quick, slow, quick, quick. I didn't think the neighbours had noticed. George had never mentioned it before.

Now looking out at the winter-beaten garden and smiling at the memories of summer, I feel the urge to start cleaning up, weeding and sowing new seed. Yep, I'll throw out the old overcoats for newer, brighter ones, as George used to say when he first taught me to prune the rose bush. And I'll say hello to the budding daffodils and tulips. Soon I'll be singing to the rhythm of the shears and doing the quick step with the rake once again. Only this year, I may even learn to dance to a different tune as I waltz to the music of an electric mower. Yes, a lawnmower – a present from my children to add to my collection of musical gardening instruments.

The Purest of Pleasures

JILL PARKER

The truth is that gardeners love gardening. Yet there is a particular variety of garden writer – a subspecies I expect, and certainly a perennial – who appears not to have grasped this vital point. 'Don't plant that one,' they say, 'it will need pruning.' 'Avoid so-and-so, you might have to water it.' I can imagine their own gardens: acres of ground smothered with impenetrable mats of dark green periwinkle. They never mention the joy of doing the actual gardening, which over-rides every discomfort and disappointment.

I admit that I had not the slightest idea of how much work I was committing myself to as I began to plant up more and more of my garden. One day I suppose I shall have to simplify, to reduce the work, but until that day comes I can indulge in the satisfaction and absorption that is like no other activity in the world. Although I must confess that for the first two seasons there was nothing in an hour's or a day's work that merited the name of gardening. Digging my way round, I filled my wheelbarrow not with weeds but with rusty barbed wire, with unearthed empty cans of hoof ointment, and other attendant constituents of farm life; some even less attractive. But these were small items to be cleared away among the expanses of stony rubble, and of course there were always the nettles which love fallen stone. Chasing the tough knots of their pink and yellow roots is one of the

46

most engrossing jobs of coarse gardening. Feeling and prodding into the ground with a fork, you can even recognise them by their distinctive smell, and I used to drag out great handfuls of next year's trouble. If in the course of unravelling you are brought up short by a wall, you can be sure the nettles will be creeping back through the crevices by next spring. For years the battle goes on, sometimes spraying the young leaf, sometimes grubbing out the old roots, and after every skirmish going in to tea with buzzing, stinging fingers – gardening gloves or no gardening gloves. After about three years of this, weeding settled down into the everyday preoccupation known to all gardeners, and it has seemed a comparative relaxation ever since my nettling experiences.

Stupidly, I have never managed to handle a hoe. Jabbing away inaccurately with the sharp edge I have wounded or even sliced through the stems of so many plants, and missed so many weeds, that I rarely use one now. At ground level though, using a trowel and my fingers, I am prepared to spend hours in hand-to-hand combat. Each type of weed has its own individual grip on the soil and one learns the tiny techniques that make them loosen their grasp. A sharp flick, a steady pull, a gentle twist or a deep scoop – all are part of the relentless tactics of hand weeding. Only to another gardener could one admit to the foolish quickening of the pulse as one follows the tenacious root of a weed, the chagrin when it breaks off and the triumph when it pulls out whole.

But the most fun in gardening can be in its variety of tasks. If I am down in the orchard, clearing a space for the little cyclamen that are getting smothered under the *Viburnum fragrans*, I might notice a damaged branch on one of the fruit trees. This needs the pruning saw that is kept in the granary but may have been left in the kitchen. In the course of that round trip I am likely to notice a dozen other jobs, some needing a moment, others an hour, all urgent and all completely different. If a peony needs a fresh stake, that's another trip to the granary. Crossing the terrace to get to the granary, I see that a recently-moved pansy is wilting and thirsty, and the watering can is over by the herb garden. Between the terrace and the herb garden, goodness knows what priorities will appear. If I am strong minded I will go straight back to the cyclamen in the orchard and begin at the beginning. But there is a delight in spending a day doing what comes next to hand in a haphazard way. It is also easier physically because you are constantly using different sets of muscles, instead of working your back, wrist or knees to the point of exhaustion. This means that by the end of the day you are aching all over instead of in one or two places, but you do recover sooner.

Pruning, though, is something I could do all day long. Naturally there are appropriate times to prune different plants but there is quite a lot one can do in the summer as well as at the beginning and end of winter. The summer-flowering shrubs are in fact the easiest to deal with because they are so perfectly consistent. To change a shrub that has finished flowering and is drooping and overblown into a clear outline of next year's promise is a constructive job undertaken in June. Following a flowered branch back, you find next year's shoot immediately behind it, all ready to grow on through the summer. A pruning cut a quarter of an inch above it gives the shoot the light and air to let it go ahead strongly. Once that is done, it is easier to see where the more ruthless pruning needs to be done – a few of the older stems that need taking out at ground level, then the weak and straggly ones, as well as any that are crossing or tangled.

By this time I tend to get trigger-happy with the secateurs, and have to stand back at a distance to take a good look. A little artistic shaping is all very well, but it is easy to get carried away and find oneself left with a sadly cropped little shrub. Spiraeas, kolkwitzias, philadelphus, weigelas – all are satisfying shrubs to prune. Once the old flowering shoots are gone one can forget that a whole year must pass before they bloom again, and look for a moment at a healthy well-shaped plant before it melts into the background. Some trick of eye and mind renders practically invisible everything in the garden whose season is done, so that one's glance slips across to the flowers whose turn is next. Provided, that is, the old shoots are pruned away, the lupins cut down, the pansies dead-headed. Fortunately the aesthetic side of this task coincides with the plants' well-being, so that their growing energy is not wasted on seeding. I wonder whether those shrubs which we grow for their autumn glamour, their seedheads or hips, would be much larger if we consistently cut them too after flowering. My *rugosa* roses, for instance, look very healthy at about five feet, but if I dead-headed them for a couple of years perhaps they would be eight feet tall. However, I doubt it. They would probably be outraged.

(No, I don't hold conversations with plants. I give them occasional instructions when I plant them, such as, 'There, you've had everything you could possibly want. Now just get on and grow.' Or if they have been damaged, and need to be trimmed back past a broken branch or stem, I do urge them, 'Try to think of it as pruning.' This sometimes works. Apart from that, it is merely a case of, 'Oh *do* try.' Or, 'Oh, well done.' That hardly counts as conversation.)

Mine is still a young garden and changing all the time. It demands constant love and attention but still insists on having its own way. It may accept or reject my efforts and it certainly makes its own rules.

What a mysterious occupation it is, making a garden!

Aching muscles and torn nails, failures and disappointments are the order of the day. So often I find myself wiping cold rain off my glasses with the corner of a muddy handkerchief. Then no sooner does the rain abate than I am told there is to be a drought. Achievements are transitory. Satisfaction is not even a word in the vocabulary, because a gardener sees with next year's eyes and is never satisfied with this year's blooms.

It is a lifelong battle, with campaigns to be mounted afresh each year against drought and ice, winds and pests, weeds and stones. Yet these are the proper background to garden life, and it is a battle without enemies and without end. Amazingly, you find yourself committed to a primrose and worrying about a pansy. Continuity is all, yet change is all, and once begun you are drawn in for life.

How is it so compelling? Why is it my favourite of all pursuits?

With the dew still on the grass on an early morning in June, a gardener may turn lyrical, and see a garden as a work of art. Work it certainly is. But what art is comparable? What work of art grows and dies, changes its appearance and asserts its own will, fades away and then returns – in fact, lives? Only a garden.

Small wonder, then, that gardening is the purest of pleasures.

From **The Purest of Pleasures**, *published by Hodder and Stoughton.*

The Orchard

DRUSILLA MODJESKA

There are some who say that Ettie's garden is a work of art. When they do, they are usually referring to Ettie's shift of allegiance from painting to gardening that came, finally and completely, with the war, and the birth of the child she gave to Helena; but it's a commonplace she greets with a frisson of unkindness, and such people are lucky if they're asked again. To call a garden a work of art, Ettie says, exposes ignorance both of gardens and of art. She says that if there is a connection then painting is a kind of gardening, not the other way round. Yet these tactless guests might be forgiven their clumsiness. Ettie reads Gertrude Jekyll's colour theory for pleasure, and her garden is poised and composed. Even in its wildest parts, where it tumbles into the gully, or along the top of the escarpment where laburnums meet banksias, and the moody oriades entwine in the maples, its shape seems coaxed to Ettie's plan. But she says in gardens, where everything is real, the uncontrollable forces of weather and season have the upper hand. The wall garden may seem a pure example of mannerism with its espalier pear, its geometric beds of herbs and lavender, its gravel paths and low box hedges, but that wall, the wall that makes it all possible, was built first and foremost to break the wind that comes gusting up from the valley. Control is always temporary, Ettie says. Provisional, contingent. Wind can change direction;

walls cannot. Plants can grow over bricks; frosts are not deterred. Which paint changes its colour from week to week, from month to month? Which composition rearranges itself within a year?

'But,' I say to Ettie's retreating back, 'gardens, like paintings, always mean something else.' She might sniff, but walking the pathways through Ettie's garden, taking whichever direction appeals, with no compulsion to travel first here, then there, following paths with their twists and turns, sudden vistas, hidden corners, it is as if one traces the course of one's own interior life, meandering through its dark corners and spectacular views, its dangers and comforts, its loves and withdrawals.

The track down to Ettie's place is steep and rocky; tourists sometimes take it by mistake thinking it's a way into the valley. When that happens Ettie opens the gate for them to turn round, and points the way back to the road that runs out on the spur where there's a car park, a lookout and steps down to the falls. For the rest Ettie's house is tucked away out of sight, a world unto itself, a sanctuary, an adytum. That's what draws people. That, and the garden.

On visits to Ettie's, one can go a whole day barely seeing her, just a glimpse of her wheelbarrow, or the sound of her boots as she comes in through the kitchen door for the next brew of tea. She likes to quote Gertrude Jekyll that a lady in the garden should be prepared for any contingency, and in particular for inclement weather. Ettie is not caught short by heat, or wind, or sudden squalls. And while she works outside with only birds and rustling creatures for company, her visitor can lie undisturbed, given over to the half-world of her verandah. Having grown up in a country where there were no such passageways between garden and house, with beds hauled out and plants growing in, the verandah has become for me an enchanted place. Neither in nor out, it holds both possibilities and excludes neither. On that verandah with its spiders and even an occasional snake, it's as if for a moment the cry and shudder of life gives way to musings that come, rolling and inconclusive, from a secretly held part of oneself. Dreaming and only half attentive, looking through strands of jasmine and wisteria that loop like curls on a great beauty's neck, towards the escarpment, it's as if, from the vantage point of a verandah bed, that great expanse of sky rolls in over us from the very edge of existence.

On other days Ettie invites her visitors to follow her down into the gully where the pond needs clearing, or to the orchard where there's pruning to be done. If I am there alone, I always go with her; but when Clara is there, I stay quietly on the verandah. 'I need a strong pair of hands,' Ettie says, and Clara sighs and lifts herself from her chair. It is then that Ettie becomes fabulist and rhetorician, telling the stories that are her real intention for rousing the girl from her reverie; not stories from her adult life, those are kept for the evenings, for Alec, the last, or should I say the most recent of her lovers, and for Louise and for me; she tells the girl the tales her Polish mother told her as they worked their way along the rows of vegetables that kept the family through the twenties, through the depression, right up to the war. She tells the girl fables about princesses with silver hands, stories of orchards laden with fruit, stories of good kings and forgetful messengers. Tangled in these tales, brought from old Europe, is the story of the loopy girl and the trees of which Ettie's mother took charge, teaching the girl to prune, filling the baskets with fruit that afterwards, after the girl had gone, Ettie would hawk around the neighbourhood. Tales of the girl's uncle, who existed in the half-light of a verandah that had become a dumping ground and storeroom, and shuffled as if he were an old man, the senses blasted out of him in another, earlier war on the other side of the world, not far from the disputed territory of Poland from which Ettie's mother had escaped, just in time. All these stories Ettie tells Clara.

But there is one story she does not tell Clara.

As a consequence Clara does not know that she is Ettie's grandchild. Very few people know the story that began with Jock in the George Street studio, long in the past, and comes into the present in the form of Clara. This is a story Louise and I are told as a secret. It is a burden that Ettie does not want handed on to another generation. What she means is that she does not want Clara burdened; and there is nothing any of us can do to dissuade her. The secret becomes ours, and she trusts us with it; the burden also.

My own desire for a garden, dormant, barely felt, was reawakened more by chance than design, as if I had to be led to it rather than make my own way there. I had no ambition to paint flowers, or to write of gardens; a garden to visit was all I required. So when Louise saw the advertisement for the house across the river, *old orchard, outhouses, fruit cage*, and rang me at Ettie's that time, I was reluctant to get on the train back to Sydney. The future seemed opaque, beyond anything I could imagine, but I went to the station, as eventually one does, and with a dreary heart let the dictates of fate convey me back to the frayed and abandoned threads of my life. As the train carried me away from the sanctuary of that mountain verandah, I had no idea how close I was to the garden that was still, then, buried in a dark corner of once-dreamed-of-desires. I could say it was just a matter of chance that Louise saw the advertisement, and that Hal already knew the valley, but as it is I don't entirely believe in chance. The question is not whether life throws up possibilities, but whether we are able to see them, and if we see them, whether we· are able to take them. There are patterns in any life, shapes and meanings that rise out of the constantly shifting possibilities of the present. To speak of luck, or of chance, is a response, sometimes envious, some-times bewildered, made by those who see others take the opportunities they miss. Or it is the self-deprecating response of those who cannot say *yes, it came to me and I risked it, I risked the whole damn thing*. Clara says this is a view of life that leaves a great deal out. Like the circumstances into which we are born; some people, she says, get dealt a mean hand. Louise says we shouldn't forget those chancy moments, those times we throw ourselves into the lap of the gods and everything falters and the gods do not necessarily smile. She says the things we give up can be as important as those we take. And I say there are times when others can see the shape of our lives more clearly than we can ourselves, and then the great act of friendship is to turn us around so that we stand to face that way.

The day after I arrived back in Sydney, Louise and I set off early for the river, driving north out of the city as the commuters drove in, out through the leafy suburbs, now so smart, where Ettie had grown up, cutting west across the scrubby plains that have been farmed into dust and consigned to chicken and car yards, and down the steep gorge that comes always with the jolt of surprise — vines, lichens, tree-ferns, stately angophoras growing from the rock, abundance once more — down to the dark silty river at the bottom, where Hal was waiting.

As the ferry ploughed slowly through the dark water, breaking up the reflection of the sky and disturbing the ducks, we leaned like figureheads against the railing. Sea gulls and river birds flipped and dipped in air currents none of us could see, belonging as they do to a spectrum that is not visible to our retinas. I stepped back and framed my hands around the two I was travelling with, framed them as if for a photo, floating out above the water, and in the stillness of that moment I felt a surge, like the kick-start of life, as they turned towards me, their eyes meeting mine in the challenge of a recognition that comes unfinished into the present.

On the other side of the river the road winds through farmland and tall stands of bush, sweet scented and elegant. I'd driven there once with Jack; but this time we turned in towards the hills, on a track that dipped and curved along the edge of a creek. When Louise pulled open the old gate at the top of the rise and Hal drove through, we all got out and stood on the ridge looking down into the shallow scoop of the valley. On the far side we could see the creek tucked in under the rocks where the hills tilt up towards the ranges behind. At a bend beneath a sheer lift of rock that shone pink in the morning sun, the creek deepens into a wide pool beside river gums. We could just make out the shape of a shack in the pepper trees where the creek turns back into open pasture. Nearer us, at the edge of the valley where the road winds down and the bush meets clear land, was the roof of the house, its tin rusting out, set in against a smooth wedge-shaped outcrop of rock. The orchard was to the left of the house in an enclosure formed by the rise of the hill on one side, the rocky outcrop, and the creek.

We drove slowly down the track to the house, a plume of dust rising behind us to mark our arrival in the silent valley. A tulip tree was growing through the verandah floorboards, wisteria had lifted its roof, birds were nesting in the eaves. But the timber was solid and the verandah's dimensions generous, shading us from the sun that was already hot on our backs. We walked through empty rooms with sagging floorboards and sooty fireplaces. We followed a path past seeded and weed-choked beds where once flowers had bloomed and vegetables thrived, past a collapsing fruit cage, a disused sheep pen where the grass grew thick and luxurious, and through a gate into the orchard. The air was still, perfumed by the early blossom and a waft of eucalypt from the bush on the hill above us. Almond trees with last year's crop rotting at their base, gnarled quinces, a magnificent greengage. Apricots, stunted apples, varieties of prunus, a single pear tree. At the centre, a huge fig.

'Some of these will have to come down,' Louise said, poking at an apricot that was rotted through.

'It'll give us room to plant more,' I said, and as I did, standing there in the silent valley where no one had lived for years, the future bloomed around me and before we'd so much as turned the first sod of earth, I could see that the garden we would make there would not be to the formal design of Ettie's, or of the gardens I had grown up with in England. There would be no box hedges and gravel paths meeting at sharp angles, no roses growing over arches, no wall to stop the winds and train the espalier pear. Here, protected by the flank of rock, and held in that shallow valley, our garden would blend itself to the shape of the land, with hollyhocks and lupins, if that's what we chose, or Sturt's desert pea and flannel flowers, edging the paths, forming banks where the ground rises, fading into shrubs, into herbs, into the shade of the verandah. No one would mistake our garden for a work of art as they do Ettie's with its mannerist certainties; and even if they did, like her I'd almost certainly reply that in gardens where everything is real, control is always temporary: provision, contingent. Meaning, of course, that it was therefore not a work of art. But secretly I would be disappointed if no one made the mistake, and paid us that compliment, for when the risks of youth become the challenge of age, one learns the provisional nature of all art, and that the existence of every painting, however certain it appears on the canvas, is always contingent. Art is created in the tension between that contingency, a necessary instability, and the order, the meaning, the pattern, that graces it. As is a garden. Or a well-lived life.

From **The Orchard,** *published by The Women's Press.*

A Gentle Plea for Chaos

MIRABEL OSLER

Looking round gardens, how many of them lack that quality which adds an extra sensory dimension for the sake of orderliness? There is an antiseptic tidiness which characterises a well-controlled gardener. And I'd go further and say that usually the gardener is male. Men seem more obsessed with order in the garden than women. They are preoccupied with flower bed edges cut with the precision of a pre-war hair cut. Using a lethal curved blade, they chop along the grass to make it conform to their schoolboy set squares, and with a dustpan and brush they collect 1 cm of wanton grass. Or, once they hold a hedge-trimmer, within seconds they have guillotined all those tender little growths on hawthorn or honeysuckle hedges that add to the blurring and enchantment of a garden in early June.

The very soul of a garden is shrivelled by zealous regimentation. Off with their heads go the ferns, ladies' mantles or crane's bill. A mania for neatness, a lust for conformity and away goes atmosphere and sensuality. What is left? Earth between plants; the dreaded tedium of clumps of colour with earth between. So the garden is reduced to merely a place of plants. Step – one, two. Stop – one, two; look down (no need ever to look up for there is no mystery ahead to draw you on), look down at each plant. Individually each is sublime undoubtedly. For a plantsman this is heaven. But where is lure? And where, alas, is seduction and gooseflesh on the arms?

There is a place for precision, naturally. Architectural lines such as those from hedges, walls, paths or topiary are the bones of a garden. But it is the artist who then allows for dishevelment and abandonment to evolve. People say gardening is the one occupation over which they have control. Fine. but why over-indulge? Control is vital for the original design and form; and a ruthless strength of mind is essential when you have planted some hideous thing you lack the courage to demolish. But there is a point when your steadying hand should be lifted and a bit of native vitality can be allowed to take over.

One of the small delights of gardening, undramatic but recurring, is when phlox or columbines seed themselves in unplanned places. When trickles of creeping jenny soften stony outlines or Welsh poppies cram a corner with their brilliant cadmium yellow alongside the deep blue spires of Jacob's ladder all arbitrarily seeding themselves like coloured smells about the place.

Cottage gardens used to have this quality. By their naturally evolved planting, brought about by the necessity of growing herbs and fruit trees, cabbages and gooseberries, among them there would be hollyhocks and honesty, campanulas and pinks. How rare now to see a real cottage garden. It is far more difficult to achieve than a contrived garden. It requires intuition, a genius for letting things have their heads.

In the Mediterranean areas this can still be seen. Discarded cans once used for fetta cheese, olives or salt fish, are painted blue or white and stuffed to overflowing with geraniums placed with unaffected artlessness on steps or walls, under trees or on a window sill. Old tins are planted with basil, they stand on the threshold of a house, not for culinary use because basil is a sacred plant, but for the aromatic pleasure when a sprig is picked for a departing traveller. Under a vine shading the well, are aubergines, melons, courgettes and a scatter of gaudy zinnias. An uncatalogued rose is grown for its scent near a seat where a fig tree provides shade and fruit. Common sense and unselfconsciousness have brought this about. A natural instinct inspired by practical necessity. We are too clever by half. We read too many books, we make too many notes. We lie too long in the bath planning gardens. Have we lost our impulsive faculties? Have we lost that intuitive feel for the flow and rightness of things; our awareness of the dynamics of a garden where things scatter where they please?

And this brings me to another observation which I think goes with my original longing for a little shambles here and there. For it seems that proper gardeners never sit in their gardens. Dedicated and single-minded the garden draws them into its embrace where their passions are never assuaged unless they are on their knees. But for us, the unserious, the improper people, who plant and drift, who prune and amble, we fritter away little dollops of time in sitting about our gardens. Benches for sunrise, seats for contemplation, resting perches for the pure sublimity of smelling the evening air or merely ruminating about a distant shrub. We are the unorthodox gardeners who don't feel compulsion to pull out campion among the delphiniums; we can idle away vacantly small chunks of time without fretting about an outcrop of buttercups groping at the pulsatillas. Freedom to loll goes with random gardening, it goes with the modicum of chaos which I long to see here and there in more gardens.

Not all gardens fail, of course. There are two for instance which have this enchantment from the moment you enter. One belongs to people I know who live on the Welsh borders, where all the cottage garden attributes such as mulberry, quince and damson trees grow amongst a profusion of valerian and chives, marjoram and sedums. The whole lush effect is immediate and soothing; it gives you a feeling of coming home, it reminds you of what life ought to be like.

In complete contrast is Rosemary Verey's garden at Barnsley House, near Cirencester in Gloucestershire. Here among the strong lines of design, parterres and walks, classical temple and knot garden, it is as if the owner had washed over the whole layout with soft, diffused colours so that hard lines are blurred. Sweet rocket and violas, rock roses and species tulips beguile, flow and confuse. It may not be chaos, it certainly isn't, but it is as if this truly cohesive effect happened while the owner had turned away her head. She hasn't, we know, for a garden like this has been painstakingly achieved from the brilliance of deliberation. Knowing when not to do things as vitally as knowing when to. There isn't a dandelion unaccounted for.

So when I make a plea for havoc, what would be lost? Merely the pristine appearance of a garden kept highly manicured which could be squandered for amiable disorder. Just in some places. Just to give a pull at our primeval senses. A mild desire for amorphous confusion which will gently infiltrate and, given time, one day will set the garden singing.

From **By Pen and By Spade: An Anthology of Garden Writing from Hortus**, *edited by David Wheeler, published by Alan Sutton.*

On Colour

I am always surprised at the vague, not to say reckless, fashion in which garden folk set to work to describe the colours of flowers, and at the way in which quite wrong colours are attributed to them. It is done in perfect good faith, and without the least consciousness of describing wrongly. In many cases it appears to be because the names of certain substances have been used conventionally or poetically to convey the idea of certain colours. And some of these errors are so old that they have acquired a kind of respectability, and are in a way accepted without challenge. When they are used about familiar flowers it does not occur to one to detect them, because one knows the flower and its true colour; but when the same old error is used in the description of a new flower, it is distinctly misleading. For instance, when we hear of golden buttercups, we know that it means bright-yellow buttercups – but in the case of a new flower, or one not generally known, surely it is better and more accurate to say bright yellow at once. Nothing is more frequent in plant catalogues than 'bright golden yellow', when bright yellow is meant. Gold is not bright yellow. I find that a gold piece laid on a gravel path, or against a sandy bank, nearly matches it in colour; and I cannot think of any flower that matches or even approaches the true colour of gold, though something near it may be seen in the pollen-covered antlers of many flowers. A match for gold may more nearly be found among dying beech leaves, and some dark colours of straw or dry grass bents, but none of these when they match the gold are bright yellow. In literature it is quite another matter; when the poet or imaginative writer says, 'a field of golden butter-cups', or 'a golden sunset', he is quite right, because he appeals to our artistic perception, and in such case only uses the word as an image of something that is rich and sumptuous and glowing.

The same irrelevance of comparison seems to run through all the colours. Flowers of a full, bright-blue colour are often described as of a 'brilliant amethystine blue'. Why amethystine? The amethyst, as we generally see it, is a stone of a washy purple colour, and though there are amethysts of a fine purple, they are not so often seen as the paler ones, and I have never seen one even faintly approaching a really blue colour. What, therefore, is the sense of likening a flower, such as a Delphinium, which is really of a splendid pure-blue colour, to the duller and totally different colour of a third-rate gem?

Another example of the same slip-slop is the term flame-coloured, and it is often preceded by the word 'gorgeous'. This contradictory mixture of terms is generally used to mean bright scarlet. When I look at a flame, whether of fire or candle, I see that the colour is a rather pale yellow, with a reddish tinge about its upper forks, and side wings often of a bluish white – no scarlet anywhere. The nearest approach to red is in the coals, not in the flame. In the case of the candle, the point of the wick is faintly red when compared with the flame, but about the flame there is no red whatever. A distant bonfire looks red at night, but I take it that the apparent redness is from seeing the flames through damp atmosphere, just as the harvest moon looks red when it rises.

And the strange thing is that in all these cases the likeness to the unlike, and much less bright, colour is given with an air of conferring the highest compliment on the flower in question. It is as if, wishing to praise some flower of a beautiful blue, one called it a brilliant slate-coloured blue. This sounds absurd, because it is unfamiliar, but the unsuitability of the comparison is scarcely greater than in the examples just quoted.

From **Wood and Garden**, *published by the Antique Collectors' Club.*

Gardening with Butterflies

MIRIAM ROTHSCHILD

I garden purely for pleasure. I love plants and flowers and green leaves and I am incurably romantic – hankering after small stars spangling the grass. Butterflies add another dimension to the garden for they are like dream flowers – childhood dreams – which have broken loose from their stalks and escaped into the sunshine. Air and angels. This is the way I look upon their presence – not as a professional entomologist, any more than I look upon roses as a botanist might – complaining that they are an impossibly 'difficult group'.

I divide my garden into three rather distinct sections. Firstly, a conventional stone-walled kitchen garden with some half-derelict glasshouses in the middle. A variety of fruit trees – morello cherries, apricots, peaches, pears, greengages and so forth are grown along the inside of the wall. Plants are cultivated in rows, in trays or in pots; the soil is a mixture of rich loams, some of it originally brought from the Bournemouth area – heaven knows why! – by goods train, around the turn of the century. After eighty years in constant cultivation with the use of an absolute minimum of sprays and insecticides, I fancy it harbours more than an average share of undesirable organisms. But that may be just an excuse when things go wrong – the 1980 epidemic of crown rot and red spider, for instance.

The second well-defined area is the house itself and the

courtyard round which it is built. Here I have planted a wide variety of creepers and wall-trained shrubs for all seasons, ranging from Japanese quince and wisteria to *Rosa banksii*, bittersweet, bryonies and varieties of clematis including traveller's-joy or old man's beard. There is a fine profusion of garden flowers and wild species where stone and soil meet round the foundations, in a sort of grassy border. A visitor arriving for the first time in this courtyard looked round at the untamed creepers and broom and the mauve and blue haze of candytuft and flax growing out of the gravel and, before ringing the bell, remarked uneasily: 'I don't believe anyone can LIVE here . . .'

Finally, the third area consists of an acre of flowering hayfield, divided from the house itself and its surrounding belt of flowers by a strip of closely cut lawn, a long bank of uncut grass and well-spaced-out wild cherry trees – by far and away my favourite tree – lilac bushes, a young ash or two, with wild honeysuckle climbing up their branches and a few crab apples, also growing in the long grass. The edges of a gravel path provide an additional mini-habitat.

Modern agricultural methods are unfortunately lethal both to wild flowers and butterflies. Cowslips and buttercups, and blue and copper wings have been cultivated, drained and bulldozed out of our fields. The smell of new-mown hay has been replaced by diesel fumes and clouds of dust, while instead of haycocks, giant circular machine-made bales stand incongruously in the fields like the droppings of some mechanical monster. But with time and trouble and exper-imentation one can get wild flowers to grow in profusion in the grass or mixed in with the good old cultivated varieties. Thus we can entice a few butterflies back into our daily lives, and hope they will dawdle and dally round the *Buddleia*.

Wordsworth, in one of his most dreadful poems, had the same thought:

> *Stay near me — do not take thy flight,*
> *A little longer stay in sight.*
> *Much converse do I find in thee*
> *Historian of my infancy.*

But you can really abandon any romantic idea of creating a *home* for these angelic creatures — the best you can do is to provide them with a good pub. And like all popular wayside inns it must have a plentiful supply of standard drinks always on tap.

Why do butterflies like some flowers more than others? Why is the taste and aroma of *Buddleia* nectar so infinitely more to their liking than the perfume and flavour of roses? We do not know. The fact is we know very little indeed about butterflies, but it is clear they prefer heavy perfume to delicate scents, and they must have the carbohydrates which they find in nectar — for flight demands a lot of energy. The plants advertise the presence of this vital food source by a delicious variety of scent and colour. The butterflies themselves exhale a delightful flowery fragrance. On a sunny day this mixture is like an umbrella of perfume spread across the garden, exciting the butterflies sexually, while the flowers are offering themselves freely in the interest of procreation. It is worth noting that where taste and smell are concerned, butterflies are superior to ourselves. They not only have chemical receptors on their tongues and antennae, but also on their feet. They can discriminate between the substance in Indian hemp which gives us a 'high' and the cannabidiol which does not, whereas to our relatively feeble nose these two are indistinguishable.

Abraham Cowley in 'The Wish' says: 'May I a small house and a large garden have', and this I believe is the right approach – even with a dearth of hands which leads inescapably to a wilderness, I doubt a garden can ever be too large. Certainly not from the butterfly's viewpoint. But so many of us are forced to be satisfied with a small patch of ground that it is an agreeable thought that butterflies can be attracted to tiny gardens as well as large ones. A *Buddleia* planted against your house, a patch of red valerian growing out of a wall, or a lavender bush constitutes a true butterfly lure. Like Alfred Tennyson, I favour 'a careless order'd garden', though growing wild flowers is no easier than cultivating the conventional, well-tried horticultural varieties. In some ways it is more difficult because not much is known about them. I doubt if you can easily find a book which tells you how to grow the lesser celandine or selfheal in a garden – or how to keep order in a little wilderness. Nor for that matter are wild flowers essential as butterfly lures, but they are a great help. Moreover it is one way of not only preserving the wild species from extinction – for who can doubt that cowslips will one day be as rare as the lady's-slipper orchid, thanks to our sprays and combines and ditching equipment – but also providing special nectar sources for butterflies.

A new type of municipal horticulture is just round the corner – when the parks in new towns, and the road verges and roundabouts will be sown with a flowering-meadow mixture instead of a dreary mono-crop of coarse grass. The rise in the price of fuel has done us one good turn – it has reduced the needless cutting of road verges and in many areas the wild flowers are already enhancing our dreary motorways. This roadside flora turns the verges into *butterfly highways* – a link between woods and nature reserves which have rapidly become like a series of oases in a desert of sprayed and smoking cornfields. Road cuttings with steep banks are ideal sunny spots for both wild flowers and butterflies. If you have a bank in your garden, cherish it.

About two hundred years ago Addison in the *Spectator* remarked that he valued his garden 'for being fuller of blackbirds than of cherries'. I agree with him, although there are times when you sigh and wish it were otherwise. Last summer I watched with mixed feelings a charm of goldfinches descend on a row of goat's-beard and pick them to pieces and rob the seed before the 'clocks' developed. I was saving them all carefully for sowing. But no one in their senses would exchange goldfinches for a row of goat's-beard, however fascinating their huge 'clocks' may be. I encourage all the birds, although bull-finches which demolish cherry and apple blossom – presumably looking for insects or even nectar? – are beautiful but pestilential and destructive creatures. And I have a passion for robins singing in the rain. I believe their songs to be outbursts of beautiful rage. . . I willingly sacrifice the odd butterfly for their sake. In a small garden you are much more conscious of insect pests, and snails, and field voles, than you are in a large one. You know each plant individually and it gets under your skin if you see your roses covered in greenfly, or the tender leaves chewed up by remorseless slugs, or half-opened cherry blossom littering the path, or foliage scalloped by leaf-cutting bees. But if you really want butterflies in the garden you have to reduce sprays to an absolute minimum and abstain from slug pellets. In my own garden, in the open, I have purchased no insecticides or weed killers or seed dressings for the last ten years, but I have sprayed diligently against fungi and green fly, in the latter case with a simple detergent, Lux, and I bring in every ladybird I can find – especially in the larval stage – and put them on the roses, hoping they will help to check the greenfly. Ladybirds, however, like butterflies, are apt to move on ... Undoubtedly the birds destroy a lot of insects, both good and bad, and in the process take their toll of flower buds and seeds. The butterflies in their turn pollinate many of my flowers, though their young stages chew up the cabbages and nasturtium (*Tropaeolum*) leaves. But by and large I give nature a free hand, and I am rewarded by the fact that I have a pair of nightingales singing close to the house and at the moment of writing thirteen species of butterflies on the wing and over a hundred species of wild flowers and grasses in the garden.

From **The Butterfly Gardener** *(with Clive Farrell), published by Michael Joseph.*

The Crossing House Garden

MARGARET FULLER

Visitors to our small garden may easily mistake the path leading between the greenhouses for the way to a service area, but those who explore further are rewarded by the discovery of a sheltered seat from which to view our secret garden. Not only secret, but also forbidden, for these twin borders, stretching as far as the eye can see, flank the busy Cambridge-to-King's Cross railway line.

A locked gate prevents visitors from trespassing on to property which belongs to British Rail and is very dangerous, so they must view it from a distance – or take a seat on one of the frequent trains and catch a fleeting glimpse, as the train rushes past, of floriferous borders and a knot garden, with terraces and seats rising out of the vegetation and busts staring out from the bushes. In the distance, pampas grass, broom, teasel and rosebay willowherb stand out from a host of cultivated and wild plants, and patches of bindweed, twitch, nettles and brambles. Piles of bricks lie about, waiting to be laid. Here and there are heaps of British Rail debris: rusty wire, chunks of concrete, fencing posts, disused sleepers, ivy-swathed telegraph poles and broken bottles lying where I have collected them, ready to be covered with compost and planted over.

To me, the garden reveals its secrets most in the hushed dawn hours of high summer when, accompanied by a mug of tea, I battle sleepily with the weeds before the heat of day brings out hordes of biting ants and flies. Looking up from unravelling goosegrass from larkspur and marigold, I am sometimes rewarded by the sight of foxes strolling across the track. Muntjak deer ignore me despite my high-visibility, BR-issue orange waistcoat. Rabbits nibble at the vegetation – no problem to me as there is plenty of greenery for all.

As the sun comes up, cuckoos, blackbirds and pigeons fill the air with a deafening chorus of welcome to the new day. When the warmth of the sun has driven away the early morning dew, lizards scuttle out from hiding places and bask in the heat on the wooden sides of a redundant chippings bin, filled now with peat and surplus calcifuge plants. Grasshoppers chirp cheerfully on the dry banks and ladybirds decorate plants like mobile jewels. Birds feed on the bounty: a flycatcher sits on his favourite fence post with a beakful of breakfast, a jay dazzles my eyes and skylarks carol merrily over the nearby fields.

Six foot of angelica suddenly rears up out of the blue geranium. A self-sown gooseberry bush provides light refreshment. Penny-royal, mint and southernwood perfume the air as they are trampled underfoot. Old-fashioned roses claw my clothing and humming bees carpet the purple thyme flowers. A myriad of seedlings jostles for light and space, bindweed thugging its way to the top, a giant grey thistle flattening competition over a square yard and reaching for the sky. The godetia needs thinning, and heavenly scented white alyssum rampages over the dry, dusty margin of a steep bank, where little else seems to flourish except for stonecrop, pinks and rock roses.

Weeding the borders is never dull – although I planted them myself, I have no idea what I am going to find next. Packets of 'Lottery Mix' seed and unnamed donations of plants and seeds from generous garden visitors ensure never-ending surprises.

Small shrubs – cotoneaster, sage, the curry plant, rue and potentilla – form the backbone of the planting, and throughout the year I gather armloads of seedling alliums, hellebores, hollyhocks and mallows and toss them along the borders – an untidy but quick way to spread them over a large area. Rather than eliminate the native plants, the more ornamental ones have been encouraged to carry on the good work of decorating the countryside. Hawthorn has been clipped into neat shapes; buttercup, speedwell, ground ivy, red deadnettle and the yellow shaving-brushes of the colts-foot are welcome in the spring. Scarlet poppies intermarry with the shirleys; lemon-yellow linaria, white campion and wild scabious fill gaps; and wild roses can be counted on to furnish the garden with a brilliant display of scarlet hips for much of the autumn and early winter. Bulbs are in their element and I am constantly dividing and replanting. Snow-drops and snowflakes relish the dry conditions, daffodils multiply and the huge red tulips I find overpowering at close quarters make a cheerful splash of colour in the distance.

In winter toads come to hibernate and bury themselves in decaying vegetation, grandfathers and little ones, to be carefully avoided by the digging fork. Then magic pervades the garden. Freezing fog creates a fairyland. Brown clumps of Michaelmas daisies and shrubs are wrapped in a sparkling shroud of glittering hoar frost laced with encrusted spiders' webs, and the borders loom in and out of sight as the fog drifts down the track. The sound of the trains is muffled to a murmur; even the missel thrush is silenced.

Perhaps the secret of the garden's sorcery is its very lack of permanence. At the moment I have lost the battle with

the weeds and the borders are reverting to a wilderness, as
British Rail has given me my marching orders.

From **Secret Gardens: Revealed by Their Owners**, *edited by Rosemary
Verey and Katherine Lambert, published by Ebury Press, Random House UK.*

The Gardens at Bilignin

ALICE B TOKLAS

For fourteen successive years the gardens at Bilignin were my joy, working in them during the summers and planning and dreaming of them during the winters. The summers frequently commenced early in April with the planting, and ended late in October with the last gathering of the winter vegetables. Bilignin, surrounded by mountains and not far from the French Alps – from higher ground a few miles away Mont Blanc was frequently visible – made early planting uncertain. One year we lost the first planting of string beans, another year the green peas were caught by late frost. It took me several years to know the climate and quite as many more to know the weather. Experience is never at bargain price. Then too I obstinately refused to accept the lore of the farmers, judging it, with the prejudice of a townswoman, to be nothing but superstition. They told me never to transplant parsley, and not to plant it on Good Friday. We did it in California, was my weak reply. They said not to plant at the moment of the new or full moon. The seed would be as indifferent as I was, was my impatient answer to this. But it was not. Before the end of our tenancy of the lovely house and gardens at Bilignin, I had become not only weather-wise but a fairly successful gardener.

In the spring of 1929 we became tenants of what had been the manor of Bilignin. We were enchanted with everything. But after careful examination of the two large vegetable gardens – the lower on a level with the terrace garden in front of the house, and the other on a considerably higher level and a distance from the court and portals – it was to my horror that I discovered the state they were in. Nothing but potatoes had been planted the year before. Poking about with a heavy stick, there seemed to be some resistance in a corner followed by a rippling movement. The rubbish and weeds would have to be cleaned out at once. In six days the seven men we mobilised in the village had accomplished this. In the corner where I had poked, a snake's nest and several snakes had been found. But so were raspberries and strawberries.

A plan was made for plots and paths. The French are adroit in weeding and gathering from paths a few inches in width. It was difficult for me to accommodate myself to them. A list of what vegetables and when they were to be planted had to be made. We had brought with us sacks of seeds of all the vegetables Gertrude Stein and I cared for and some with which we would experiment. To do the heavy work a boy from the hamlet had been found. After fertilisers had been turned into the ground and the topsoil raked to a powder, with a prayer the planting commenced. The seeds for early gathering had scarcely been disposed of when it was time to plant the slips bought from farmers' wives in the square at Belley at the Saturday-morning market. There were two horticulturists in Belley. But the slips we had from them were not all vigorous; we planted twice as many as we intended to grow.

The wind blew the seeds from the weeds in the uncultivated fields that surrounded the gardens. The topsoil was of made earth and heavy rains commenced to wash it away. These were the two disadvantages we should have to overcome. The weeds remained a tormenting, backbreaking experience all the summers we spent at Bilignin. After the autumn gathering was over, the topsoil would be renewed. Fortunately there was plenty of water. Only once was there a drought, when the ox carts brought water in barrels from the stream in the valley below. For watering we had bought three-hundred feet of hose.

The work in the vegetables — Gertrude Stein was undertaking for the moment the care of the flowers and box hedges — was a full-time job and more. Later it became a joke, Gertrude Stein asking me what I saw when I closed my eyes, and I answered, Weeds. That, she said, was not the answer, and so weeds were changed to strawberries. The small strawberries, called by the French wood strawberries, are not wild but cultivated. It took me an hour to gather a small basket for Gertrude Stein's breakfast, and later when there was a plantation of them in the upper garden our young guests were told that if they cared to eat them they should do the picking themselves.

The first gathering of the garden in May of salads, radishes and herbs made me feel like a mother about her baby — how could anything so beautiful be mine? And this emotion of wonder filled me for each vegetable as it was gathered every year. There is nothing that is comparable to it, as satisfactory or as thrilling, as gathering the vegetables one has grown.

When autumn came, the last harvest was so occupying that one forgot that it meant leaving the garden for the return to Paris. Not only did the winter vegetables have to be gathered and placed to dry for a day before packing, but their roots and leaves had to be put on the compost heap with manure and leaves and packed down for the winter. The day the huge baskets were packed was my proudest in all the year. The cold sun would shine on the orange-coloured carrots, the green, yellow and white pumpkins and squash, the purple egg-plants and a few last red tomatoes. They made for me more poignant colour than any post-Impressionist picture. Merely to look at them made all the rest of the year's pleasure insignificant. Gertrude Stein took a more practical attitude. She came out into the denuded wet cold garden and, looking at the number of baskets and crates, asked if they were all being sent to Paris, that if they were the *expressage* would ruin us. She thought that there were enough vegetables for an institution and reminded me that our household consisted of three people. There was no question that, looking at that harvest as an economic question, it was disastrous, but from the point of view of the satisfaction which work and aesthetic confer, it was sublime.

From **The Alice B Toklas Cookbook**, *published by Michael Joseph.*

Sairam's Garden

MANJU KAK

Every morning as I crept out, dishevelled in my dressing-gown, my tea-less mouth dry, to fetch the paper at our doorstep, I would see him. In rolled up pyjamas, hose in hand, he would be watering his plants with serious intent. I envied him his garden that first year. Ours had no hedge, just torn, scraggly bushes, more broken in places than mending. Across the gate, his stalwart, well-trimmed mehndi grew thicker and thicker, green and luxuriant. My few bushes were mere lantana. The poor things never looked upward and I wished I could scold them, pull their arms up, or hang them from the curtain rails till they stretched.

The truth was our garden was limp when we moved in to our new home in Delhi. The lawn was like a bit of rag. The flower-beds lay empty. I wanted a good garden. I just wasn't quite sure how to go about it. I tried to tell my husband. 'Trust your intuition,' was all he said. So we planted a few seedlings, watered and pulled out weeds occasionally.

To my surprise, the garden gradually started perking up. But my euphoria was short-lived. A few weeks later, a push-cart drew up next door at Sairam's and unloaded eight glossy crotons in tropical hues, five banana plants, three montesaria and a dozen variety of fern. (Yes, I admit I counted the lot!) All were in their prime, and found pride of place on his front porch.

My perky new shoots began to look dismal in comparison. 'It's no use,' I told my husband. 'You can't make a garden like this. Planting from scratch! It'll take months before any of it grows. It's six months since we moved in and . . . and . . . why even his lawn looks more mowed!'

I gazed enviously at the lush green that swathed Sairam's porch. The fine mehndi hedge and the well-demarcated flower-beds. Sairam, our neighbour, was definitely orderly. He used imported seeds from a special shop, hoses and pipes of quality PVC. Even the green iceberg lettuce heads in his vegetable garden were dazzling. Naturally, I felt sour.

As October approached, we planted our winter seeds and seedlings. We got them from here and there, from friends and work-mates, and they went in everywhere, filling every spare bit of ground. Flower seeds were scattered alongside the vegetables, in the borders and in between rows, even in the little patches where the monsoon cauliflower had fought shy and not budded. We planted and positioned diligently, our hands caked with mud and our clothes rimmed with dirt, till night sucked in the foggy light of dusk and it was too dark to work any more. When it was all over, I remarked somewhat caustically, 'I wonder what Sairam will have to say to this!'

I soon found out when Sairam came along one morning after the planting was done.

'Ahaa,' he said, surveying the little shoots, already sprouting tall, their limpness abandoned astonishingly early. 'So you have poppies, cosmos and calendula there. Calendula! Hardy plants!' And he twitched his long nose. 'Nothing really remarkable about them though. Too yellow, I think. Cornflower. Aaah – *Centaurea cyanus* – now there's a decent flower, stays in bloom. But among tomatoes? Have you thought of planting some antirrhinum, *Hibiscus rosa sinenus* or *Celosia cristata*? They're all worthy plants.'

I just nodded, impressed by his knowledge of Latin names.

'See what I mean,' I said to my husband later, 'We should have gone about it the proper way.'

'Doesn't matter,' he muttered lazily, stretching flat on the divan, a newspaper pitched over his eyes. 'All we wanted were some flowers, right?'

But it worried me, all that I didn't know.

All was not lost however, I reasoned. There was next year to think of. I made trips to the library and in place of my usual novels, I picked up books on gardening instead. Before going to sleep, I'd switch on the bedside light and read out gardening tips late into the night.

Meanwhile, winter came. My blooms were a bit late. January passed and they were still in the process of budding. Then, one day in February we woke to see the first poppy push a tentative head out of its bursting green casing. Two days later, a mass of them burst into flower with an exuberance that gladdened. Blood-red petals with velvety skins that I caressed. I raced in with the newspaper to shake my husband out of his slumber.

'We have flowers!' I cried.

He tumbled out of bed and we dragged cane chairs into the garden, the dog yapping at our feet. A pot of tea and we sat through the hour, saying nothing.

A week later, it was the cornflowers' turn. And in the days that followed, others came. Like Roman columns, the colours marched on. First came the cosmos batallion, then the flocks, the dahlias, the asters, the sweet william and the candytuft. California poppies shone like bright bits of sunshine between the rows of sylvan green spinach. Every morning there were more blooms, each successive wave pushing earlier ones aside to make room for themselves and bask in our admiration. Until finally we were completely surrounded by glowing colour.

Came March with its early warnings of the dry heat of summer and there were still flowers and more flowers clustered between the pale heads of cabbage, spirals of tomato and dusty leaves of aubergine. Rows of flame-coloured nasturtium seemed to climb out from everywhere, throwing darting sap-green tendrils into the mint, lettuce and fenugreek.

Wandering out one dawn with my cup of tea, I saw Sairam with his hose, still conscientiously watering his budding heads and careful rows of subdued green. I drew closer to our common boundary.

'Your blooms?' I asked.

'Yes, a bit late,' he replied, tight-lipped as he continued showering the recalcitrant plants.

'They'll come, they'll come,' I murmured, already feeling the searing winds of April upon us.

'Hmmm,' he nodded.

'Perhaps it's the shade of the neem tree?' I consoled.

'Possibly,' he said crisply.

I turned to walk back when I was confounded. I still don't believe what I saw. Was it a trick of the eye or my imagination in the cheeky green buds thumbing their noses at him?

Never Spray Against Greenfly

MAUREEN AND BRIDGET BOLAND

There is a giant conspiracy between the insecticide manufacturers and writers on gardening to encourage the public to spend fortunes and waste hours spraying their roses against aphids. A single clove of garlic planted beside each rose is guaranteed by the present writers (who have not been bought by the lobby – though perhaps only because they have never been approached) absolutely to keep greenfly from the plant. The roots will take up from the soil a substance from the garlic inimical to greenfly, and if in early spring a few hatch out from eggs of parents careless of their offspring's welfare they will neither lay nor survive themselves. Whatever it is that the rose takes up from the garlic does not affect its own scent, and so long as the garlic is not allowed to flower there will be no odour of garlic in the garden. Try it for one year with one group of roses in one bed protected only by garlic, spraying all the others in the garden as much as you need, and you will never waste money or time again. All members of the onion family, including chives, are partially effective, but garlic is the only completely efficient answer, the systemic insecticide to end all others. In very dry weather, water the garlic so that the excretions from its roots will be sure to be taken up by the thirsty rose.

From **The Complete Old Wives' Lore for Gardeners**, *published by The Bodley Head.*

Woman's Place

ELEANOR PERÉNYI

There are the husband's apple and pear trees, twined by the wife's clematis; his cabbage beds fringed with her pinks and pansies; the tool-house wreathed with roses; his rougher labour adorned by her gayer fancy, all speaking loudly of their hearts and tastes ... We trust the cottager's wife will love and care for the flowers and we are sure if she does that her husband's love and esteem for her will be heightened and strengthened.

From an English gardening magazine, 1848

A charming sentiment on the face of it, but what about that veiled threat at the end? Why should the cottager's love and esteem for his wife be contingent on her care for the flowers? And if he neglected the apple and pear trees – would she then be entitled to think less of *him*? It may come as a surprise that sexism should play any part in horticulture but the more you read of gardening history the more convincing the case for it becomes, and the less you are ready to see the cottager as a chivalrous male doing the hard work while indulging his wife in her 'gayer fancy'. Divisions of labor there have been, but not nearly as simple as that, while the whole business of women's supposed devotion to flowers may need another look.

At Woburn Abbey in the seventeenth century there was

a famously lifelike statue of a woman weeding, and records
of English estates show that from a very early period this
chore was almost exclusively performed by females. It is, says
my source (who is, naturally, a man), 'a task at which they
have always been pre-eminent,' and this is an assessment with
which male gardeners have long agreed. La Quintinie, who
was in charge of Louis XIV's *potagers* and otherwise an ador-
able person, recommended the hiring of married men rather
than bachelors (as was the usual custom), on the ground that
wives would be available for weeding, as well as cleaning and
scraping out pots. In the Orient, women weed the rice
paddies in water up to their knees. In general, it is to be
observed that men plow while women sow; prune fruit and
nut trees but leave the harvest to women; and most men like
working with vegetables (all, that is, but the weeding). Other
crops appear to be largely in the hands of women. In that
part of Turkey where tobacco is grown, I saw them patting
together the raised beds, setting out seedlings, and of course
weeding, while the male population sat under pergolas
playing tric-trac. But why pick on Turks? In other parts of
the world women are thought to be pre-eminent at hauling
brushwood on their backs. Russian grannies sweep leaves in
parks and streets.

Altogether, it is pretty obvious that relative physical
strength isn't the determining factor in most cases of divided
labor but rather which tasks men prefer to do and which
they have decided to leave to women. The man in charge
of our Hungarian vineyard was the envy of the neighborhood
on account of his ten terrific daughters, who could and did
get through twice the work of any male, and he didn't
hesitate to lay it on them. In peasant societies nobody worries
very much about overtaxing women's strength. I doubt if
they do in any society. What men fear is competition and

losing the services of women as drudges. Thus, La Quintinie must have known that women could be trained as well as men to perform a hundred more exacting and interesting horticultural tasks than scraping out pots.

This is all the more striking when you consider that it was women who invented horticulture in the first place, women who ventured into field and forest in search of wild plants, and women who domesticated them while men were still out chasing wild beasts. Women were the first gardeners; but when men retired from the hunting field and decided in favor of agriculture instead, women steadily lost control. No longer were they the ones to decide what was planted, how, or where; and accordingly the space allotted to them diminished too, until flowers and herbs were the only plants left under their direct management, while their former power passed into myth. The inventor of agriculture became the goddess of agriculture, her daughter the bringer of spring, when plants come to life; and each of these had a flower or flowers assigned to her – almost certainly by men and as a form of propitiation. For make no mistake: Men were always half in a terror of women's complicity with nature, and the power it had given them. The other face of the goddess belongs to the witch brewing her spells from plants, able to cure and also curse with her knowledge of their properties. In some societies this fear of women amounted to panic. It was believed that their mere presence could blight vegetation. Democritus wrote that a menstruating woman could kill young produce 'merely by looking at it'. On the one hand, the benign giver of life and fertility; on the other, the baneful caster of withering spells – it's a tall order and no wonder that men were inclined to confine such a dangerously two-faced influence to a safe place.

For that is how I have come to interpret the two-thousand-odd years of women's incarceration in the flower garden. The superstitious fear that women were in league with nature in some way that men were not was thus simultaneously catered to and kept in check. Flowers are of all plants the least menacing and the most useless. Their sole purpose is to be beautiful and to give pleasure – which is what one half of man wants from woman (the other, it is needless to say, asks for qualities more practical and down-to-earth) – and as such they are the perfect combination of tribute and demand. A gift of flowers to a woman implies that she is as deliciously desirable as the blossoms themselves; but there may be another and hidden message, contained in old-fashioned phrases like 'shy as a violet,' 'clinging vine,' not originally conceived as pejoratives, that tells more of the truth – which is that flowers are also emblems of feminine submission. In the western world, this is rarely explicit. In the Orient, where fewer bones are made about the position of women, two examples may be cited. The art of Japanese flower arrangement, *ikebanu*, whose masters are male, was originally imparted to women as a means of silent communication with stern samurai husbands to whom words, and especially plaintive words, would have been an intolerable presumption; whereas an iris and a pussy willow and perhaps a convolvulus, arranged in the right order, conveyed a world of meaning. In China, we find another example, one that borders on the atrocious: the bound foot, to be encountered as late as the 1920s. My Chinese amah's feet were bound, and filled me with fascinated horror. What unspeakable distortion lay inside that delicate little slipper that caused her to sway (seductively to men, that was the point) as she walked? She would never show me but I have seen photographs since, and learned that the hideously crushed mass of flesh and bone was compared by Chinese poets to a lotus bud.

With this in mind, one may feel that those paintings of Chinese gardens in which exquisitely clad ladies float about tending to potted peonies depict scenes less idyllic than they appear. What we are seeing is a sort of floral cage – one that in the Hindu and Moslem world was an actual prison. Purdah and the harem were mitigated for their captives by the presence of many beautiful flowers. The illiterate women in the Ottoman seraglio even devised a 'language of flowers' (described with some scorn by Lady Mary Wortley Montagu in her letters from Turkey and later all the rage among European females with nothing better to do) to take the place of the written language forbidden them. But there was no escape from the famous tulip gardens of the seraglio. Call them what you will – and as everybody knows the word 'paradise' derives from the Persian word for garden, an idea later expanded in Moslem usage to mean a heaven where male wants were attended to by ravishing and submissive houris – one of the principle functions of the Oriental garden from Turkey to China was the incarceration of women.

To equate European gardens with any such purpose might seem to carry feminist interpretation too far, and obviously the differences are great. Garden plans never the less suggest a similar if less drastic impulse on the part of men. The Roman atrium was a flower-filled enclosure chiefly for women's use, and it is in marked contrast to the pleasure grounds laid out by a rich Roman gentleman and intellectual like Pliny, who makes it perfectly clear that his were entirely for male diversion. Those pavilions for reading and sunbathing, dining with friends, those philosopher's walks, were for himself and his male companions. Possibly there was somewhere an inner courtyard where the women of the household could spend their leisure time, and more than likely it was filled with flowers, if only those that would be picked for the house; but except for his violet beds, he doesn't speak of flowers – or of women.

Medieval gardens repeat the pattern of the *hortus conclusus*, with the difference that they are more elaborate and better adapted to feminine comfort. Trellised walks, turf seats, tiny flower beds, all mark a female presence that is borne out in the illuminations and tapestries where we almost invariably see a lady stooping to pluck a strawberry, a rose, or at her ease with embroidery and lute. So plainly were they designed for women that they even convey an illusion of female supremacy at last – and it wasn't entirely an illusion. The mass folly of the Crusades occupied European men for the better part of two hundred years, and with her lord away at the wars the chatelaine did often manage his estate at home, and not badly either. She lived behind fortified walls never the less, and it isn't hard to conjecture that her garden was in the nature of a chastity belt, locking her in until the return of her lord and master. 'A garden inclosed is my sister, my spouse; a spring shut up, a fountain sealed,' says the Song of Solomon – to all of course but him. That feminine purity is only to be preserved within four walls is another ancient idea, and in the late Middle Ages it found indirect expression in those curious paintings of so-called Mary gardens, which show the Virgin seated in a castellated enclosure surrounded by richly symbolic fruits, vines and flowers. But the fortified walls came down with the return of something like peace and leisure, and the Renaissance garden with its magical perspectives, its cascades and fountains, was another story altogether – a celebration of humanism – except that in Italy at least it always had an odd little appendix attached, as it were, to the grand design: the *giardino segreto*.

Garden histories don't try to account for the *giardini segreti* except to note that flowers, largely absent in the rest of the garden, grew in them. To me it is at least plausible that these fossilized remnants of the medieval garden were for women, intended to be so, and that in fact they kept alive the tradition of the flower-filled feminine ghetto.

'Know that it doesn't displease but rather pleases me that you should have roses to grow and violets to care for,' wrote a fifteenth-century French merchant to his wife, sounding the note to be heard again and again for the next three hundred years. From 1500 to 1800 was the great age of garden design: visions of what a garden should be shifted like scenery upon a stage, theories multiplied and books on the subject poured from the presses. But in England only two were in all that time specifically directed to women, and both assume her province to be flowers and herbs. Lawson's *Countrie Housewife* (1618) gives her a list of sixteen flowers for nose-gays, five kinds of bulbs including 'Tulippos,' and twenty-six herbs. Charles Evelyn's *Lady's Recreation* (1707) discusses most of the same flowers while permitting a fountain and 'an excellent contriv'd statue'. He also allows her a wilderness where 'being no longer pleas'd with a solitary Amusement you come out into a large Road, where you have the Diversion of seeing Travellers pass by, to compleat your Variety.' Why she should be solitary and driven to watch travellers in the road he doesn't say. His whole tone, however, is one of a patronage that is echoed elsewhere. Sir William Temple (*Garden of Epicurus*, 1685): 'I will not enter upon any account of flowers, having only pleased myself with seeing or smelling them, and not troubled myself with the care, which is more the ladies' part than the men's . . .' John Lawrence (*New System . . . a Complete Body of Husbandry and Gardening*, 1726) adds to patronage something like a scolding:

'I flatter myself the Ladies would soon think that their vacant Hours in the Culture of the *Flower-Garden* would be more innocently spent and with greater Satisfaction than the common Talk over a Tea-Table where Envy and Detraction so commonly preside. Whereas when Opportunity and Weather invite them amongst their Flowers, there they may dress, and admire and cultivate Beauties like themselves without *envying* or *being envied.*' Here the argument for keeping women shut up with flowers is almost entirely trivialized. The Virgin's bower is now a school for decorum.

What amazes me is the way female scholars have failed to notice the implications of statements like these. Eleanor Sinclair Rohde (*The Story of the Garden*, 1932), to whom I am indebted for many of my quotations, gives no hint that she catches their drift. She takes no umbrage at her adored Parkinson (or perhaps doesn't choose to understand him) when she quotes a passage like this from the *Paradisus*: 'Gentlewomen, these pleasures are the delights of leasure [*sic*], which hath bred your love and liking to them, and although you are not herein predominant, yet cannot they be barred from your beloved, who I doubt not, will share with you in the delight as much as is fit.' Not the cleanest prose in the world, and Mrs Rohde construes it as a tribute to the central place of women in seventeenth-century gardening. I read it as the opposite: a warning to wives with ideas about garden layout to leave that area to their husbands, who know best but will, if not aggravated, allow a share in the result.

Whichever of us is right, history is on my side. Not until the twentieth century did any woman play a recognizable part in garden design. We know why, of course. The great gardens of the world have been reflections of men's intellectual and spiritual experience: visions of Arcadia, hymns to rationalism or the divine right of kings, Zen parables – and the well-known reasons for our failure to compose symphonies, paint masterpieces, conceive the Einstein theory, apply equally to our failure to produce a feminine incarnation of, say, Le Nôtre. One or two great gardens *were* made for women, who were queens or the equivalent; but as they were always in the prevailing fashion it isn't possible to tell to what extent they conformed to the client's particular wishes. In one case we know they didn't. Marie de Medici's ideas for the Luxembourg were resolutely opposed by her designer, the incomparable Boyceau, and he had his way (much to posterity's gain, it should be said). We know, too, that Marie Antoinette's *hameau*, arranged in what she imagined to be the English style, was done in a taste all her own, but that sad spot, so out of place at Versailles, doesn't say much in favor of feminine theories about design.

Malmaison might be a happier example. It, too, was laid out for a woman, and given the Empress Josephine's character, one can be sure she got what she wanted. Malmaison, however, isn't outstanding for its design but for the millions of roses that grew there, probably the greatest collection the world has ever seen; and this was generally true of all gardens made by or for women of which we have any record. Flowers were, and until the twentieth century remained, the theme. In the eighteenth century, the Duchess of Beaufort grew exotics, as did Mme de Pompadour in all the many ravishing gardens given her by Louis XV – she adored the white, highly scented tropicals, gardenias and jasmine especially, brought to her from all parts of the French empire. Lady Broughton specialized in alpines, and was one of the first to grow them outdoors in a rock garden; Lady Holland introduced dahlias to England and grew them in her greenhouses.

Here, a new note was introduced, for it was at about this

time that women were allowed to embark on the study of botany – not too seriously and rather late in the day; and it is notable that various writers should have seen their studies in much the same light as pottering in the flower garden itself. J C Loudon, for one, recommended botany as 'a charming and instructive female exercise,' or a grade or two above the netting of purses, and in the hands of the upper-class young ladies who went in for it, that was about what these studies amounted to. In fact, they mostly consisted in the coloring of flower engravings, and counting stamens according to the newly introduced Linnaean system of classification, which made everything wonderfully simple. Honorable exceptions there were, mostly royal. The dowager Princess of Wales founded the great botanic garden at Kew in 1761; and Queen Charlotte was accounted a passionate student, though how she found time for her researches in the course of bearing her sixteen children is a wonder. The *Strelitzia* or bird-of-paradise flower, however, is named for her (she was born Mecklenberg–Strelitz), as were four varieties of apple – hence, it is said, Apple Charlotte, the dessert.

Women in humbler positions, who might have contributed rather more to the science, did not fare so well. One of them was Jane Colden, the daughter of a lieutenant-governor of New York, who lived near Newburgh-on-Hudson and who ventured into the wilderness at a time when that was neither easy nor safe. By 1758 she had compiled a manuscript describing four hundred local plants and their uses, illustrated by herself. It was never published. During the Revolution it fell into the hands of a Hessian officer who was interested in botany. He took it back to Germany where it was preserved at the University of Göttingen. Evidently it was important enough to have been purchased at a later date by Sir Joseph Banks, the most influential botanist of his time; but he didn't try to have it published and it reposes in the British Museum to this day. Nor is any flower called *Coldenia*, the accolade regularly bestowed by botanists on those of their tribe who have made important contributions to science. (That those standards have been less than strict is, however, obvious even where men's names are concerned: The *Montanoa*, a species of shrub, appears to have been named for a Mexican bandit-politician. As applied to women, names seem chiefly to have been bows to rank: *Victoria amazonica*, that water-lily whose pad is the size of a dinner table, was of course named for the dear queen; while the *Cinchona*, from whose bark quinine is derived, was called after the Condesa de Cinchon, Vicerene of Peru, who in 1638 was cured of malaria by a decoction of what had previously been called Peruvian bark.)

Given the circumstances – circumscribed travel, the reluctance to admit that female minds could cope seriously with science – it isn't surprising that no woman made a name for herself in botany. That her accomplishments in the breeding and cultivating of plants should also be a well-kept secret is another matter. 'In March and in April from morning till night/In sowing and seeding good housewives delight,' sang Thomas Tusser (1524–80) in his rhyming calendar for gardeners. Even in Tudor times England was famous for the beauty of its flowers, especially doubled varieties – columbines, primroses, violets, marigolds and campanulas – but also striped and unusual colors, which included sports such as a reddish lily-of-the-valley. Foreigners attributed these variations to the damp English climate which allowed for year-around planting, but also noted that the selection and cultivation were done by housewives rather than professionals – at that period well behind their French and Dutch colleagues. In the seventeenth century, the great age of English plantsmanship, when collectors like the Tradescants began to range the world, these accomplishments receded into the background – where they remained for another two hundred years. What the Victorians called 'old-fashioned' flowers were really housewives' flowers, grown continuously and in defiance or ignorance of fashion – including the landscape movement that destroyed so many of England's finest and most characteristic gardens and prohibited so much as a cowslip from showing its pretty head above ground. In the feminine domain called the cottage garden, which a modern state might designate as a preserve with plants whose removal would be punishable by law, grew such otherwise lost rarities as blue primroses, Parkinson's 'stately Crown Imperial,' and the fairy rose (not to be confused with the modern polyantha of that name), many violas and pinks long since vanished from cultivation in the gardens of the rich and those desiring to be à la page.

The cottage garden was rediscovered towards the end of the nineteenth century – mostly by women like Mrs Juliana Horatia Ewing, who founded a Parkinson Society 'to search out and cultivate old flowers which have become scarce,' and of course Gertrude Jekyll, who reintroduced the fairy rose. But although these gardens clearly pointed to the role of women as important conservators as well as breeders and cultivators of plant species, no one pursued the obvious conclusion that what had happened in the nineteenth century might also be presumed to have occurred in others as well. No writer I know of has, for example, enlarged the thesis that in the Dark Ages it was monks in monasteries who preserved such species as survived in those parts of Europe not fortunate enough to be conquered by the garden-loving Arabs (Spain, Sicily, etc.). Why not also nuns in nunneries? It is known that they grew flowers in profusion for the adornment of churches and herbs for simples, just as the monks did. Indeed it was one of their functions to school ladies in the uses of cooking and medicinal herbs (which then included flowers like marigolds, poppies, even roses and honeysuckle), especially the latter because it was the lady of the manor who compounded and administered medicines, though she wasn't of course honored with the title of physician, and the few venturesome women who did try to set themselves up as doctors were promptly squelched.

With all the vast amount of writing about gardens that has appeared in the last hundred years, much of it by women, you might expect somebody to have devoted a book to women's place in gardening history. If anyone has, I haven't heard of it, and it must be admitted that the difficulties of research would be formidable. Where would the documentation come from? In England, the earliest herbal published by a woman was Elizabeth Blackwell's in 1737. The earliest essay on gardening itself is probably Lady Charlotte Murray's *British Garden* (1799); in America, Mrs Martha Logan's *Gardener's Kalender* (known only through republication in a magazine around 1798). What the library stacks of other countries would yield I can't say; the pickings would presumably be even slimmer. Private correspondence would be a richer source, if one knew where to look. (There are, for instance, tantalizing hints in Mme de Sévigné's letters that in the age dominated by Le Nôtre's geometry she had ideas about *la nature* that anticipated Rousseau's — as when she told her daughter that she had spent the morning on her country estate 'in the dew up to my knees laying lines; I am making winding *allées* all around my park . . .') Novels by women could also be studied in this light. Jane Austen has a great deal about the theory and practice of gardening, especially in *Mansfield Park*, where a part of the plot hinges on Mr Rushworth's determination to have Mr Repton remodel his grounds, though in fact every novel has its gardens and each is made to say something about the character and social situation of the owner. (Elizabeth Bennet isn't entirely joking when she says she must date her falling in love with Mr Darcy to her visit to his 'beautiful grounds at Pemberley'.)

Diaries and notebooks would be another source, not forgetting *The Pillow Book of Sei Shōnagon*. In the remoter past, the body of feminine knowledge was locked away under the anonymous heading of old wives' tales, a phrase I have always found offensive. Assume that 'old' doesn't mean the woman gardener was a crone but refers to 'old times'. The expression still implies a combination of ignorance and superstition peculiarly female – and never mind that a thirteenth-century church father like the Abbott of Beauvais testified that a decoction of heliotrope could produce invisibility or that St Gregory the Great believed the devil hid in lettuce heads. Women will have shed their superstitions at about the same time men did, and what many an old wives' tale really refers to is orally transmitted information, as often as not the result of illiteracy, not inborn backwardness. Women weren't stupider than men; they lacked the means of expressing themselves, and instead of writing herbals or treatises on what is called (note this) husbandry, they told one another what experience had taught them about plants, medicines and many other things. This is also called folk wisdom, and it can be as discriminatory as the rest of human history: How many people know, for instance, that the subtly constructed tents of the Plains Indians were designed and set up entirely by women?

To remedy these deficiencies wouldn't be easy, but I wish somebody would try. The story could end well, too – up to a point. In the spring of 1980 a symposium was held at Dumbarton Oaks whose subject was 'Beatrix Jones Farrand (1872–1959) and fifty Years of American Landscape Architecture'. The setting was appropriate: Mrs Farrand designed the beautiful garden at Dumbarton Oaks and many other famous ones as well. She was the only woman among the eleven original members of the American Society of Landscape Architects, founded in 1899, and the first to demonstrate that women could design gardens as well as plant flowers. (Jekyll, remember, worked in collaboration with the architect Edwin Lutyens.) She was a thorough professional and inaugurated a period of great brilliance for women as landscape architects. Ellen Biddle Shipman, another of them, told a reporter in 1938 that 'until women took up landscaping, gardening in this country was at its lowest ebb. The renaissance was due largely to the fact that women, instead of working over their boards, used plants as if they were painting pictures and as an artist would. Today women are at the top of the profession.'

That, alas, is no longer true. Not only are the gardens designed by those women for the most part in a sad state of neglect, the profession itself leaves something to be desired. It has, so it seems, gone back to the drawing boards. Many universities now separate courses in design and horticulture into different academic departments. We are where we were in earlier centuries when the designer and the plantsman lived in different worlds – an extraordinary step backward. Does it also represent a resurgence of male chauvinism, a return of the old idea that flowers and plants are a province less worthy than that of stone and water? Not overtly so perhaps. But the lack of interest in horticulture shown by liberated women, including liberated women architects, suggests that they recognize, however subconsciously, the link between flowering plant and old-style femininity as opposed to feminism, and if forced to choose between the two courses, as I gather the students more or less must, would opt for the 'higher' (i.e., male-dominated) one of landscaping. If so, though we have come a long way from the statue of the female weeder and the cottager's wife, it isn't far enough.

From **Green Thoughts: A Writer in the Garden**, *published by Viking Penguin.*

In Search of Our Mothers' Gardens

ALICE WALKER

In the late 1920s my mother ran away from home to marry my father. Marriage, if not running away, was expected of seventeen-year-old girls. By the time she was twenty, she had two children and was pregnant with a third. Five children later, I was born. And this is how I came to know my mother: she seemed a large, soft, loving-eyed woman who was rarely impatient in our home. Her quick, violent temper was on view only a few times a year, when she battled with the white landlord who had the misfortune to suggest to her that her children did not need to go to school.

She made all the clothes we wore, even my brothers' overalls. She made all the towels and sheets we used. She spent the summers canning vegetables and fruits. She spent the winter evenings making quilts enough to cover all our beds.

During the 'working' day, she labored beside – not behind – my father in the fields. Her day began before sunup, and did not end until late at night. There was never a moment for her to sit down, undisturbed, to unravel her own private thoughts; never a time free from interruption – by work or the noisy inquiries of her many children. And yet, it is to my mother – and all our mothers who were not famous – that I went in search of the secret of what has fed that muzzled and often mutilated, but vibrant, creative spirit that the black woman has inherited, and that pops out in wild and unlikely places to this day.

But when, you will ask, did my overworked mother have time to know or care about feeding the creative spirit?

The answer is so simple that many of us have spent years discovering it. We have constantly looked high, when we should have looked high – and low.

For example: in the Smithsonian Institution in Washington, DC, there hangs a quilt unlike any other in the world. In fanciful, inspired, and yet simple and identifiable figures, it portrays the story of the Crucifixion. It is considered rare, beyond price. Though it follows no known pattern of quilt-making, and though it is made of bits and pieces of worthless rags, it is obviously the work of a person of powerful imagination and deep spiritual feeling. Below this quilt I saw a note that says it was made by 'an anonymous Black woman in Alabama, a hundred years ago.'

If we could locate this 'anonymous' black woman from Alabama, she would turn out to be one of our grandmothers – an artist who left her mark in the only materials she could afford, and in the only medium her position in society allowed her to use.

As Virginia Woolf wrote further, in *A Room of One's Own*:

Yet genius of a sort must have existed among women as it must have existed among the working class. [Change this to 'slaves' and 'the wives and daughters of sharecroppers'.] Now and again an Emily Brontë or a Robert Burns [change this to 'a Zora Hurston or a Richard Wright'] blazes out and proves its presence. But certainly it never got itself on to paper. When, however, one reads of a witch being ducked, of a woman possessed by devils [or 'Sainthood'], of a wise woman selling herbs [our root workers], or even a very remarkable man who had a mother, then I think we are on the track of a lost novelist, a suppressed poet, of some mute and inglorious Jane Austen . . . Indeed, I would venture to guess that Anon, who wrote so many poems without signing them, was often a woman . . .

And so our mothers and grandmothers have, more often than not anonymously, handed on the creative spark, the seed of the flower they themselves never hoped to see: or like a sealed letter they could not plainly read.

And so it is, certainly, with my own mother. Unlike 'Ma' Rainey's songs, which retained their creator's name even while blasting forth from Bessie Smith's mouth, no song or poem will bear my mother's name. Yet so many of the stories that I write, that we all write, are my mother's stories. Only recently did I fully realize this: that through years of listening to my mother's stories of her life, I have absorbed not only the stories themselves, but something of the manner in which she spoke, something of the urgency that involves the knowledge that her stories – like her life – must be recorded. It is probably for this reason that so much of what I have written is about characters whose counterparts in real life are so much older than I am.

But the telling of these stories, which came from my mother's lips as naturally as breathing, was not the only way my mother showed herself as an artist. For stories, too, were subject to being distracted, to dying without conclusion. Dinners must be started, and cotton must be gathered before the big rains. The artist that was and is my mother showed itself to me only after many years. This is what I finally noticed:

Like Mem, a character in *The Third Life of Grange Copeland*, my mother adorned with flowers whatever shabby house we were forced to live in. And not just your typical straggly country stand of zinnias, either. She planted ambitious gardens — and still does — with over fifty different varieties of plants that bloom profusely from early March until late November. Before she left home for the fields, she watered her flowers, chopped up the grass, and laid out new beds. When she returned from the fields she might divide clumps of bulbs, dig a cold pit, uproot and replant roses, or prune branches from her taller bushes or trees — until night came and it was too dark to see.

Whatever she planted grew as if by magic, and her fame as a grower of flowers spread over three counties. Because of her creativity with her flowers, even my memories of poverty are seen through a screen of blooms — sunflowers, petunias, roses, dahlias, forsythia, spirea, delphiniums, verbena . . . and on and on.

And I remember people coming to my mother's yard to be given cuttings from her flowers; I hear again the praise showered on her because whatever rocky soil she landed on, she turned into a garden. A garden so brilliant with colors, so original in its design, so magnificent with life and creativity, that to this day people drive by our house in Georgia — perfect strangers and imperfect strangers — and ask to stand or walk among my mother's art.

I notice that it is only when my mother is working in her flowers that she is radiant, almost to the point of being invisible — except as Creator: hand and eye. She is involved in work her soul must have. Ordering the universe in the image of her personal conception of Beauty.

Her face, as she prepares the Art that is her gift, is a legacy of respect she leaves to me, for all that illuminates and cherishes life. She has handed down respect for the possibilities – and the will to grasp them.

For her, so hindered and intruded upon in so many ways, being an artist has still been a daily part of her life. This ability to hold on, even in very simple ways, is work black women have done for a very long time.

This poem is not enough, but it is something, for the woman who literally covered the holes in our walls with sunflowers:

> They were women then
> My mama's generation
> Husky of voice – Stout of
> Step
> With fists as well as
> Hands
> How they battered down
> Doors
> And ironed
> Starched white
> Shirts
> How they led
> Armies
> Headragged Generals
> Across mined
> Fields
> Booby-trapped
> Kitchens
> To discover books
> Desks
> A place for us
> How they knew what we
> Must know

> *Without knowing a page*
> *Of it*
> *Themselves.*

Guided by my heritage of a love of beauty and a respect for strength — in search of my mother's garden, I found my own.

From **In Search of Our Mothers' Gardens,** *published by The Women's Press.*

Sido

COLETTE

In her garden my mother had a habit of addressing to the four cardinal points not only direct remarks and replies that sounded, when heard from our sitting-room, like brief inspired soliloquies, but the actual manifestations of her courtesy, which generally took the form of plants and flowers. But in addition to these points – to Cèbe and the rue des Vignes, to Mother Adolphe and Maître de Fourolles – there was also a zone of collateral points, more distant and less defined, whose contact with us was by means of stifled sounds and signals. My childish pride and imagination saw our house as the central point of a Mariner's Chart of gardens, winds, and rays of light, no section of which lay quite beyond my mother's influence.

I could gain my liberty at any moment by means of an easy climb over a gate, a wall, or a little sloping roof, but as soon as I landed back on the gravel of our own garden, illusion and faith returned to me. For as soon as she had asked me: 'Where have you come from?' and frowned the ritual frown, my mother would resume her placid, radiant garden-face, so much more beautiful than her anxious indoor-face. And merely because she held sway there and watched over it all, the walls grew higher, the enclosures which I had so easily traversed by jumping from wall to wall and branch to branch became unknown lands, and I found myself once more among the familiar wonders.

'Is that you I hear, Cèbe?' my mother would call. 'Have you seen my cat?'

She pushed back her wide-brimmed hat of burnt straw until it slid down her shoulders, held by a brown taffeta ribbon round her neck, and threw her head back to confront the sky with her fearless grey glance and her face the colour of an autumn apple. Did her voice strike the bird on the weathercock, the hovering honey-buzzard, the last leaf on the walnut-tree or the dormer window which, at the first light, swallowed up the barn owls? Then – though it was certain to happen, the surprise was never failing – from a cloud on the left the voice of a prophet with a bad cold would let fall a: 'No, Madame Colê . . . ê . . . tte!' which seemed to be making its way with great difficulty through a curly beard and blankets of fog, and slithering over ponds vaporous with cold. Or perhaps: 'Ye . . . es, Madame Colê . . . ê . . . tte!', the voice of a shrill angel would sing on the right, probably perched on the spindle-shaped cirrus cloud which was sailing along to meet the young moon. 'She's he . . . e . . . ard you. She's go . . . oing through the li . . . i . . . lacs.'

'Thank you!' called my mother at random. 'If that's you, Cèbe, just give me back my stake and my planting-out line, will you! I need them to get my lettuces straight. But be careful. I'm close to the hydrangeas!' As if it were the offering of a dream, the prank of a witches' sabbath, or an act of magical levitation, the stake, wound round with ten yards of small cord, sailed through the air and came to rest at my mother's feet.

On other occasions she would offer to lesser, invisible spirits a tribute of flowers. Faithful to her ritual, she threw back her head and scanned the sky: 'Who wants some of my double red violets?' she cried.

'I do, Madame Colê ... ê ... tte!' answered the mysterious one to the East, in her plaintive, feminine voice.

'Here you are, then!' and the little bunch, tied together with a juicy jonquil leaf, flew through the air, to be gratefully received by the plaintive Orient. 'How lovely they smell! To think I can't grow any as good!'

'Of course you can't,' I would think, and felt inclined to add: 'It's all a question of the air they breathe.'

No one could equal Sido, either, at separating and counting the talc-like skins of onions. 'One ... two ... three coats; three coats on the onions!' And letting her spectacles or her lorgnette fall on her lap, she would add pensively: 'That means a hard winter. I must have the pump wrapped in straw. Besides, the tortoise has dug itself in already, and the squirrels round about Guillemette have stolen quantities of walnuts and cob-nuts for their stories. Squirrels always know everything.'

If the newspapers foretold a thaw my mother would shrug her shoulders and laugh scornfully. 'A thaw? Those Paris meteorologists can't teach me anything about that! Look at the cat's paws!' Feeling chilly, the cat had indeed folded her paws out of sight beneath her, and shut her eyes tight. 'When there's only going to be a short spell of cold,' went on Sido, 'the cat rolls herself into a turban with her nose against the root of her tail. But when it's going to be really bitter, she tucks in the pads of her front paws and rolls them up like a muff.'

All the year round she kept racks full of plants in pots standing on green-painted wooden steps. There were rare geraniums, dwarf rose-bushes, spiraeas with misty white and pink plumes, a few 'succulents', hairy and squat as crabs, and murderous cacti. Two warm walls formed an angle which kept the harsh winds from her trial-ground, which consisted of some red earthenware bowls in which I could see nothing but loose, dormant earth.

'Don't touch!'

'But nothing's coming up!'

'And what do you know about it? Is it for you to decide? Read what's written on the labels stuck in the pots! These are seeds of blue lupin; that's a narcissus bulb from Holland; those are seeds of winter-cherry; that's a cutting of hibiscus – no, of course it isn't a dead twig! – and those are some seeds of sweet-peas whose flowers have ears like little hares. And that . . . and that . . .'

'Yes, and that?'

My mother pushed her hat back, nibbled the chain of her lorgnette, and put the problem frankly to me:

'I'm really very worried I can't remember whether it was a family of crocus bulbs I planted there, or the chrysalis of an emperor moth.'

'We've only got to scratch to find out.'

A swift hand stopped mine. Why did no one ever model or paint or carve that hand of Sido's, tanned and wrinkled early by household tasks, gardening, cold water, and the sun, with its long, finely-tapering fingers and its beautiful, convex, oval nails?

'Not on your life! If it's the chrysalis, it'll die as soon as the air touches it, and if it's the crocus, the light will shrivel its little white shoot and we'll have to begin all over again. Are you taking in what I say? You won't touch it?'

'No, mother.'

As she spoke her face, alight with faith and an all-embracing curiosity, was hidden by another, older face, resigned and gentle. She knew that I should not be able to resist, any more than she could, the desire to know, and that like herself I should ferret in the earth of that flowerpot until it had given up its secret. I never thought of our resemblance, but she knew I was her own daughter and that, child though I was, I was already seeking for that sense of shock, the quickened heart-beat, and the sudden stoppage of the breath – symptoms of the private ecstasy of the treasure-seeker. A treasure is not merely something hidden under the earth, or the rocks, or the sea. The vision of gold and gems is but a blurred mirage. To me the important thing is to lay bare and bring to light something that no human eye before mine has gazed upon.

She knew then that I was going to scratch on the sly in her trial-ground until I came upon the upward-climbing claw of the cotyledon, the sturdy sprout urged out of its sheath by the spring. I thwarted the blind purpose of the bilious-looking, black-brown chrysalis, and hurled it from its temporary death into a final nothingness.

'You don't understand . . . you can't understand. You're nothing but a little eight-year-old murderess . . . or is it ten? You just can't understand something that wants to live.' That was the only punishment I got for my misdeeds; but that was hard enough for me to bear.

Sido loathed flowers to be sacrificed. Although her one idea was to give, I have seen her refuse a request for flowers to adorn a hearse or a grave. She would harden her heart, frown, and answer 'No' with a vindictive look.

'But it's for poor Monsieur Enfert who died last night! Poor Madame Enfert's so pathetic, she says if she could see her husband depart covered with flowers, it would console her! And you've got such lovely moss-roses, Madame Colette.'

'My moss-roses on a corpse! What an outrage!'

It was an involuntary cry, but even after she had pulled herself together she still said: 'No. My roses have not been condemned to die at the same time as Monsieur Enfert.'

But she gladly sacrificed a very beautiful flower to a very small child, a child not yet able to speak, like the little boy whom a neighbour to the East proudly brought into the garden one day, to show him off to her. My mother found fault with the infant's swaddling clothes, for being too tight, untied his three-piece bonnet and his unnecessary woollen shawl, and then gazed to her heart's content on his bronze ringlets, his cheeks, and the enormous, stern black eyes of a ten-months-old baby boy, really so much more beautiful than any other boy of ten months! She gave him a *cuisse-de-nymphe-émue* rose, and he accepted it with delight, put it in his mouth, and sucked it; then he kneaded it with his powerful little hands and tore off the petals, as curved and carmine as his own lips.

'Stop it, you naughty boy!' cried his young mother.

But mine, with looks and words, applauded his massacre of the rose, and in my jealousy I said nothing.

From **My Mother's House and Sido**, *translated by Enid Mcleod, published by Secker and Warburg Ltd.*

Letter to Her Daughter

SIDO

Sir,

You asked me to come and spend a week with you, which means I would be near my daughter, whom I adore. You who live with her know how rarely I see her, how much her presence delights me, and I'm touched that you should ask me to come and see her. All the same I'm not going to accept your kind invitation, for the time being at any rate. The reason is that my pink cactus is probably going to flower. It's a very rare plant I've been given, and I'm told that in our climate it flowers only once every four years. Now, I am already a very old woman, and if I went away when my pink cactus is about to flower, I'm certain I shouldn't see it flower again.

So I beg you, sir, to accept my sincere thanks and my regrets, together with my kind regards.

> *Sidonie Colette (Colette's mother),*
> *to her son-in-law*
> *written when she was seventy-six;*
> *she died a year later.*

From **Break of Day**, *translated by Enid Mcleod, published by Secker and Warburg Ltd.*

A Flower-Arranging Summer

MAY SARTON

Making a garden is not a gentle hobby for the elderly, to be picked up and laid down like a game of solitaire. It is a grand passion. It seizes a person whole, and once it has done so he [*sic*] will have to accept that his life is going to be radically changed. There are seasons when he will hesitate to travel, and if he does travel, his mind will be distracted by the thousand and one children he has left behind, children who are always in peril of one sort or another. However sober he may have been before, he will soon become an inveterate gambler who cuts his losses and begins again; he may think he intends to pare down on spending energy and money, but that is an illusion, and he soon learns that a garden is an ever-expanding venture. Whatever he had considered to be his profession has become an avocation. His vocation is his garden.

How lucky it is for me, then, that Nelson is far enough north so there are four months of the year when there is nothing to be done outdoors! By late November the garden has been put to bed and will sleep until late April. Snow-bound, I can at last concentrate on writing. But when the day's stint is done I pore over seed catalogues and the brochures of nurserymen, and dream of next year's garden. So, at least in my imagination, the garden is very much alive all the time . . . as with any other grand passion.

When Céline and I planted those first perennials, I had no idea what I was getting myself in for, for I had never had a garden of my own. But I did recognize the symptoms of the vocation from living near my mother, who could not inhabit and apartment for even a few months without taking over a little plot of earth under a porch or alongside a back entrance and making it flower.

From May on, I can hardly wait to get up to see what has happened overnight, for one of the pleasures of a garden is that something is always happening; it is not static, even for a day. I go out by six-thirty and sometimes earlier, still in my pyjamas and a wrapper, to take a look around before breakfast. Perhaps the hummingbird has come back and I'll catch a glimpse of the ruby throat as he flashes past and, like me, pauses at each flower. It sometimes seems as if each plant had its bird. The goldfinches love cosmos; the cedar waxwings too. The hummingbird is a great delphinium-drinker, and when that is gone stays on as long as nicotiana is in flower.

This early morning walk around the garden is contemplative. It is not a time to work but rather a time to taste the air, and not only to look at the flowers but to look out beyond the tamed world to the long meadow and the great trees beyond it, for they too are always changing. A most delightful thing about this garden is the wilderness it lies in, a small orderly pocket in a vast natural world. The present cats – two speckled sisters – sense the difference just as I do. Beyond the garden they creep in and out of the long grasses and among the daisies like tigers, but as soon as one of them is inside the garden proper, she comes to sit decorously under a rosebush, paws tucked in and wearing the expression of Queen Victoria at her most bland.

How much hope, expectation, and sheer hard work goes

into the smallest success! There is no being sure of anything except that whatever has been created will change in time, and sometimes quite erratically. And, like parents whose children suddenly shoot up beyond them, I am always being taken by surprise. Those peonies in the big border are huge now, bearing perhaps fifty swanlike flowers each. But they have crowded out smaller plants. When the iris is at its most splendid, an army of white, gold, purple, and blue standards, the wary gardener knows that it is time to divide it. What is to be done with the basketfuls left over?

It never crossed my mind when I started that one of the joys would be to have plants to give away. But now two or three neighbors' gardens have flowered to new richness on my iris. In exchange I have been given lovely bits of theirs – a white rugosa rose that Mildred dug up for me one day; the loveliest lilac I have, deep purple, that Quig brought over early one morning and laid beside my back steps. I set it in right there, and there, every spring, it flowers in Quig's name.

The first half hour of the morning I spend enjoying the air and watching for miracles. After breakfast I spend an hour or more arranging and rearranging seven or eight bunches of flowers for the house. There are flowers indoors here all the year around – in winter, bowls of narcissus, geraniums brought in from the window-boxes in the autumn, cut flowers from a local florist when all else fails. But from late May on I have variety to play with, and the joy becomes arduous and complex. Arranging flowers is like writing in that it is an art of choice. Not everything can be used of the rich material that rushes forward demanding utterance. And just as one tries one word after another, puts a phrase together only to tear it apart, so one arranges flowers. It is engrossing work, and needs a fresh eye and a steady hand. When you think the thing is finished, it may suddenly topple over, or look too crowded after all, or a little meager. It needs one more note of bright pink, or it needs white. White in a bunch of flowers does a little of what black does in a painting, I have found. It acts as a catalyst for all the colors. After that first hour I have used up my 'seeing energy' for a while, just as, after three hours at my desk, the edge begins to go, the critical edge.

One of the things gardening does for me is to provide a way of resting without being bored; a day divided between writing in the morning and gardening in the afternoon has a good balance; it is possible to maintain what might be called perfect pitch, total awareness, for a good many hours of such a day. And gardening is so rich in sensuous pleasures that I hardly notice its solitariness.

Flowers and plants are silent presences; they nourish every sense except the ear . . . and that subtle observer Elizabeth McClelland once wrote of the 'creaking' of the tulips, so even hearing may be involved. What a pleasure it is to touch the hairy bud of a poppy, or to pick up the velvety fallen petal of a rose, or to get a wave of sharp sweetness from the peony bed as one goes past! One cannot eat these glories, but I often pick a raspberry or two while I am working, or chew a mint leaf or a sprig of parsley. Plants do not speak, but their silence is alive with change.

For the joys a garden brings are already going as they come. They are poignant. When the first apple falls with that tremendous thud, one of the big seasonal changes startles the heart. The swanlike peony suddenly lets all its petals fall in a snowy pile, and it is time to say goodbye until another June. But by then the delphinium is on the way, and the lilies . . . the flowers ring their changes through a long cycle, a cycle that will be renewed. That is what the gardener often forgets. To the flowers we never have to say goodbye forever. *We* grow older every year, but not the garden; it is reborn every spring.

Like any grand passion, my garden has been nourished by memory as well as by desire, and is a meeting place, an intersection, where remembered joys can be re-created. I first saw shirley poppies – and if I had to choose only one flower, I might choose them – in Basil de Selincourt's garden near Oxford, in the Cotswolds. Basil sowed shirley poppies on a long bank a little above a more formal perennial border; and when they flowered, a diaphanous host, shaken by the light and wind, playing their endless variations on the themes of pink, white, and red, they were a wonder to behold. Everything about this flower is magic – its curious hairy stem; the tightly folded petals, a little damp, that open out of nothing like Fortuny dresses, to show the shaggy crown of gold or black stamens; and finally the intricate turret of the seed pod. So when my shirley poppies flower, it is Basil who comes back with them.

I first saw fritillaries – the flower, not the butterfly – by a brook at Penns in the Rocks, where the poet Dorothy Wellesley lived. The house took its name from a miniature mountain of wild rocks and trees near where it stands, in a hollow, as if they were both sunk in dream, as was the poet herself in her old age. There the ghost of Yeats was never very far away, the atmosphere all of legend as one climbed up to a small Grecian temple built in his memory at the top of the hill. The fritillaries broke into this dreamlike visit into the past with their vivid present. Could they be real, these tiny lanterns, chequered purple and white, opening to a bell with as sharply chiseled petals as in a child's drawing of an imaginary flower? They *were* real, and now they spring up here under an old forsythia bush, year by year, to evoke Yeats and DW – as if I should ever forget them.

Two Chinese peonies speak to me always of Ellery Sedgwick, being wheeled out in his last years to sit and contemplate·one after another of these beauties, an old man whose exuberant delight flew out from him as if it were a flotilla of butterflies, to rest on this flower or that – a winged *attention* he gave also to those he loved, to poetry, to creation itself. Ellery, I miss you! But I find you again every June when the peonies are in flower.

My mother's light ghost is everywhere in my garden, of course, but there are certain times and certain places where I am more aware of her presence than usual. One time is October when I am on my knees for hours planting bulbs on every sunny day, for this was one task I often helped her with, the silver-gray cat, Cloudy, playing wildly among the leaves beside us, and the whole atmosphere one of hope. At the moment of planting a bulb, all is hope, no dismay. Then, there is surely something hauntingly symbolic about burying a living thing toward a sure resurrection, at a moment in the season when everything else is dying or on the way out. I order bulbs extravagantly, as I now know that more than half will make a chipmunk's winter bearable. But no matter what the casualties, in October the vision of massed tulips and daffodils is there in the mind's eye.

In the middle of the garden at Channing Place there was a patch of 'wild wood', and here my mother planted trillium and bluebells. I was inspired to do the same in a patch of 'wild wood' below the terraced gardens after Ruth Harnden came up from Plymouth with pink lady's-slippers from her woods and planted them there in my absence. Her gift suggested a new place to 'expand' into. So last year I planted a hundred bluebells down there. Will they spread, and eventually make a blue pool in memory of Mabel Sarton? Who knows? A garden is a perpetual experiment. It may evoke, but it can rarely memorialize, at least in the sense of imitation. Gardens are as original as people.

My mother is most with me as a living presence when I go out to weed. What better way to get over a black mood than an hour of furious weeding! That violent tearing up and casting away of the dreadfully healthy weeds also tears up and casts away the dreadfully healthy demons – and my mother had her demons too. Clearing away all that stifles and distresses tender plants to give them air and space clears away at the same time all that has been stifling the person. How often I have seen my mother come in from such a battle flushed with joy. There, in her garden, she balanced a rich and sometimes anguished temperament against tough reality, and there, she, so frail in some ways, plagued by illness, learned how to survive.

Yes, gardening gives one back a sense of proportion about everything except itself. What a relief it was to me when I read that Vita Sackville-West kept a pile of metal labels in a shed at Sissinghurst as proof of all the experiments that had failed! I had, until then, been ashamed of how much waste there was even in my unpretentious garden here. I blamed inexperience, impatience, and extravagance. But now I have come to accept that one must not count the losses, they would be too alarming. One must count only the joys, and feel continually blessed in them. There is no unlucky gardener, for each small success so heavily outweighs each defeat in his passionate heart.

Two years ago, the dwarf plum trees by the kitchen door flowered for the first time. Is there a more haunting presence than plum? It is sweet, but not too sweet, a little spiced, sweetness with a shade of bitterness in it. I remember getting out of the train at Enka-Kuji, a Zen monastery not far from Tokyo, on a chill March day, and being taken by surprise. What was that incense? It was plum blossom.

Now it was here, right at my door. I could look out on two clouds of white, supported on black irregular twigs, and alive with bees. The next morning the oriole came to shine his orange flame among all those white petals. I could hardly believe it. I had heard the oriole more than once, but I had not actually seen one since that first day when I came to look at the house and he had appeared don the maple like an angel. Yes, it was true. The oriole had come back to celebrate the first flowering of the plum, and perhaps also to celebrate much else that had seemed a wild dream and has come true in the last six years.

Is there a joy except gardening that asks so much, and gives so much? I know of no other except, perhaps, the writing of a poem. They are much alike, even in the amount of waste that has to be accepted for the sake of the rare, chancy joy when all goes well. And they are alike in that both are passions that bring renewal with them. But there is a difference: poetry is for all ages; gardening is one of the late joys, for youth is too impatient, too self-absorbed, and usually not rooted deeply enough to create a garden. Gardening is one of the rewards of middle age, when one is ready for an impersonal passion, a passion that demands patience, acute awareness of a world outside oneself, and the power to keep on growing through all the times of drought, through the cold snows, toward those moments of pure joy when all failures are forgotten and the plum tree flowers.

From **Plant Dreaming Deep**, *published by The Women's Press.*

Urban Gardening for the Soul

KIRAN GREWAL

It was during my early childhood that I first became aware of the importance of urban gardening as a reminder to those of us who lived in inner-city areas of the essential beauty and healing power of flowers and plants – those 'hyacinths of the soul' which can transform even the dullest concrete and brick environments. We lived in a large first-floor apartment in a suburb of Nairobi beyond which lay the wilderness that was Nairobi National Park. On the balcony, my mother had planted some exotic passionflowers in tubs. These strange flowers fascinated me and watering them became a favourite ritual which I have recreated in my own urban garden today – the window-box.

When I was nine, my family went to live in India for two years – in a region of the Punjab, my father's birthplace. I spent hours gazing at the dry landscaped gardens of contemporary India, with its concrete, grass and fountains everywhere, rather like the nineteen-fifties' setting of a Jacques Tati film in its homage to modern architecture. Like Jacques Tati, we were not quite sure how to enjoy these sophisticated unnatural spaces.

During those constant sunshine days, my playmates and I would step gingerly on the sparse grass, more used to playing in the corridors of the house or on the streets. Inevitably, we would end up on the flat rooftops of our homes – the few potted plants providing minor explosions of colour under the relentless blue skies. The peace and quiet of the roof was other worldly; the sense of space something precious away from the hustle and bustle of the street.

In my early teens came the domestic aesthetic influence of the gardens of England, first viewed under a thick mantle of powdery snow, the pewter sky outlining large shrubs and trees. Looking out from the windows of our new, semi-detached home in a London suburb, I was moved by the exotic bleakness of the wintry English garden. The clothes line swaying in the wind above abandoned bikes and bright, plastic children's toys in our shrouded, white backyard was at once comforting and alien. Come summer, our next-door neighbours tended their runner beans and sweet peas with great care, smiling proudly at the healthy plants.

My father and I always disagreed about the role and function of the garden. He was Mr Lawnmower Man. Although I too loved using the rusty red-and-blue manual mower, whirring noisily as it chopped up the bright, tender green blades, I preferred the wildness of the too-long grass. When he decapitated the young oak and apple trees, he went too far. I went into mourning, sad that I would not see the leaves changing colour through the seasons, green to red, gold and rusty brown. Dad came from a farming background and like a farmer felt no remorse at having to destroy so he could grow something different and more profitable. Still, treeless and bleak though it looked in the winter, during the summer, I had to grudgingly accept that the garden with its new plants had taken off successfully, especially the wild profusion of pink roses growing in an arc over the narrow piece of lawn near the garden shed.

That rickety old garden shed became my very own private den, a place to escape to and dream. Once, while still in my teens, it was the only place my boyfriend and I could think of to spend the night, unable as we were to be together at either of our homes. I can still remember the two of us huddling together, listening to the rain pattering down on the wooden roof. My father, needless to say, was furious when he discovered us there in the morning.

The garden provided an extension of my life beyond that of the suburban semi-detached interior I inhabited. It represented a promise of endless possibilities, but also held the warning of a stifling, conventional existence in its landscape. There was a world to explore beyond the garden shed; London was calling.

I was twenty-four when I first moved in to my own inner-city flat after four years of sharing as a student. It was on the fourth floor of a tenement block of hard-to-let council flats with brown, hessian-covered walls. Although glad to have my own space and a roof over my head, I felt as if I were entombed in brick and concrete. The only thing that gave me hope was a window-box full of dry earth and dead roots, forgotten on the window sill. In my daydreams, I imagined it in its full glory, thick with foliage and deep-red, orange and white flowers. It sprung to life, the archetypal window-box, just as I had seen in photographs from all over the world, from downtown Tokyo to the Swiss Alps.

But it was winter – and no plants could survive the harsh winds and cold. None the less, the roofs of Kennington needed immediate obscuring. So I got busy, cutting out plants with big yellow and red flowers from multi-coloured cellophane. Pasting these on the window gave a stained-glass effect, and as the daylight filtered through, my instant urban garden lifted my spirits and hid the brick-and-concrete view.

As lead skies turned gradually to blue, the flat rooftops of my new home reminded me of those of my Indian childhood. I was determined to gain access, and managed to persuade the caretaker to part company with the key which opened the door at the top of my stairwell. Accompanied by my friends from art school, I turned the lock eagerly, full of anticipation. As we stepped out on to the large, flat expanse, we could hardly contain our excitement as our first sight immediately confirmed how brilliant it was. We looked around, grinning madly. The liberation of space was breathtaking. Even the less-than-thrilling South London environs below failed to dampen our spirits. In the distance lay the buildings and towers of the City of London. St Paul's Cathedral to the east and Crystal Palace to the south. On the wind came the faint chimes of Big Ben striking the hour, its pale clock-face only partially obscured by chimney pots.

The roof was a wonderful discovery, almost like finding a secret garden, a place for the imagination to run riot. I even fantasised briefly about putting turf down so we could graze goats and keep chickens in central London. Needless to say, this vision did not come to pass. The only animal that had obvious access was a pet dog, judging by the clues left behind, along with piles of old junk, in one corner of the roof. By and large, though, it was clear that no one ventured up here much.

The uniqueness of the space, however, made me want to use it. But while the thought of cultivating a roof garden was a pleasurable fantasy, its realisation demanded hard work. Instead, one summer's day, after painting the floorboards white in the flat, inspiration struck. There was plenty of paint left so why not use it creatively on the roof? Loud post-punk music blared as three art students armed with paintbrushes began to tackle the brick chimney faces that edged my roof top. I went for Tunisian palm trees – after all, if you can't have the real thing, why not paint it? Peter, my comrade-in-arms, went for a wild, primitive, expressionist abstract, his sweepingly dramatic brushstrokes made all the more striking by the contrast of white against the dark grey of the main chimney wall. Martin, the third member of our party, was kept busy bringing up more paint and frantically rolling cigarettes, almost in time to the music.

Having access to that enormous canvas under a beautiful sunny-blue sky was a wonderful experience. And having painted, make-believe trees was definitely better than having blank walls. Plus, my new plants needed practically no maintenance. As dusk fell, we viewed our work with pride, drunk on the knowledge that we'd created a virtual garden, without having to wait for the plants to grow. Our instant, urban non-garden became the place to be. A place to escape to and feel the sun on your face during the day; a place for loud, wild parties at night.

However, my window-box still beckoned, and with summer upon us it was time to take action. I found myself looking enviously at other people's wonderfully blooming boxes, and sighing. I wondered if the baskets hanging outside my local pub would be missed. I was practically broke, and there was no money available for buying plants. The only option, it was decided, was to go to the nearby wholesale plant-and-flower market that opened at five in the morning. We took Pro-plus, drank tequila, played Monopoly and argued animatedly all night just so we would be among the first customers at dawn, and could buy the best plants available at trade prices. As daylight broke through the darkness, we walked to the market, feeling very fragile and emotional.

Being surrounded by a sea of green leaves and a myriad of flowers in intense hues eased our hangovers as we bartered over the best deals. Then armed with our trays of young plants, we had full fry-up breakfasts of mushrooms, eggs and bacon, washed down with beer, at the pub where the market traders ate. It was a place of strange, underworld activity, secret handshakes and tatooed, muscular men.

Buying plants for the window-box in summer has become a ritual over the years. I'd buy bright red geraniums with velvet petals – hardly adventurous, but every time I'd look at the colour they provided, I felt quite happy and less deprived of a real garden. However, it has become increasingly difficult to walk past a florist without being seduced by the plants on sale, and wondering if it wouldn't be too extravagant to buy another for the window-box. On one occasion, I tried replacing my geraniums with fuchsias, but to my deep disappointment, it was too windy and the delicate flowers soon wilted and dropped off. I've also toyed with the idea of having two small conifers, but somehow have never managed to find the right ones.

Instead, one summer's day last year, I was moved to paint a huge pink flower on the last remaining empty wall on the roof, a virtual flower-garden of triffid proportions. My neighbours probably put it down to post-art-school dementia. They had actually succeeded in creating a 'real' urban garden, lugging big plant pots on to the roof, and transforming the space into a very pleasant place to be.

All of us city-dwellers long for some green space, an escape from the noise, concrete and traffic fumes. Unfortunately, having never had the money – or determination – to create a 'real' urban garden, the most I have managed in the circumstances is the cultivation of my window-box and my painted, imaginary oasis on the roof. But I would feel buried alive without these gardens to enjoy. And, apart from the therapy that all my 'acts' of gardening provide, the ironically postmodern aspect of this non-gardening delights me too.

Soon it will be time to begin my yearly replenishing of

the window-box, which currently sports one hardy geranium from last summer. This year, it will be the red-and-white variegated variety, plus two small conifers and a miniature rose. Or perhaps I should plant a passionflower in my garden? For I am also planning to invest in a shiny aluminium watering can so that I can really get into the act of gardening – just as I did as a child, tending to my mother's plants on the balcony in Nairobi.

Enter a Non-Gardener

OLIVE PITKIN

'I'm not going to garden,' I said firmly. I never *had* gardened; I had never even seen any gardening done, to speak of. It was true that my parents had a vegetable plot in the backyard in Vermont, about twenty by thirty feet, where they raised all the vegetables our family ever ate. But they didn't believe in child labour and my only recollections of how it was done concerned a compost pile behind the garage (the nearest my mother could come to the manure pile of her farm youth) and the backbreaking toil of spading the whole area up every spring. I did remember, also, seeing my mother bring out water to her young tomato plants in July, dipping a careful pint or so around each one. This was all 'gardening' meant to me and it did not appeal to me either as recreation or food supply. Those tomatoes were good, though, hot from the vine . . . and the young peas on the Fourth of July. . . But I wanted none of it. I had enough to do.

It became apparent pretty promptly, though, that we had to do *something*, here and there. You can't just sit on your deck and admire the greenery all the time; sometimes you like to move around a little and get a different view. Moving around on our property that first summer was something to be undertaken with machete in hand. The children took a shortcut to the north, across the golf course, to get to their tennis lessons, and that involved traversing a 20–foot expanse of mixed blueberries, bayberries, and roses. Not agreeable. I myself, in order to get to a stone suitable for leaning-against-with-poetry-book, had to wade through underbrush in a way that was not always convenient. Poison ivy was a constant danger, and we very soon found out that we were all 'susceptible' to it.

So paths had to be cleared. I made one through that northernmost strip of scratchy scrub and two more leading up to it, one from each side of the house. I had not, at that time, read anything about the layout or design of paths (and as for the *construction* of paths, I would have thought it a contradiction in terms – and still do); but they turned out to be properly meandering because they had to go around big rocks and because it was easier to cut them through the least dense shrubbery.

Then the house looked awfully raw and square, sitting on its thin new patch of lawn. It had about a foot of exposed foundation, which didn't help. So, on our trips to the North Stonington town dump (we hadn't yet discovered the much closer local dump), which was located on a most beautiful wooded hillside, I dug up bunches of ferns and stuck them in around the house. A few wildflowers caught my eye and I stuck them in on the somewhat sunnier west side.

When I say 'I stuck them in', that's just what I did. My one tool was a trowel and with it I would make a hole just big enough to hold the transplantee, shove the plant in, and push the soil back around it. Sometimes I watered them afterwards (remembering my mother's care for her tomatoes), sometimes I didn't – reasoning that because they were wild and tough they'd thrive under any abuse.

They didn't. The ferns were all right (I've since found that you can't kill a fern short of putting it in a live furnace), but the wildflowers mostly died or sat there, one by one in a straight line, looking totally pathetic and usually refusing to bloom. The ones that did bloom appeared to be doing so as an act of desperation and, having given their all, would then die. By the end of our first year these plantings could best be described as hopeless.

There was all that poison ivy to deal with. There was the raw, steep bank to the west of the house, where the space for its foundation had been gouged out of the hillside. There was that nice stretch of land sloping down to the road below the house, giving seductive intimations of woodsiness, but, in its native state, altogether baffling human entry.

And finally, once I had become a bit used to the overall aspect of greenery, there was the undeniable fact that it could stand some improvement – that in fact it demanded improvement in order to be truly picturesque and usable. I had no intention of turning our country hideaway into a suburban plot, and I really *didn't* want to garden. But, I felt as I gazed and gazed, our little bit of land was not being its best self. While it was undoubtedly a diamond, it was also undoubtedly very much in the rough. Those nice groups of bayberries, for example – they were festooned with various drooping vines and creepers and disfigured by fountains of high sea-grass around their trunks. Many of the cedars had dead branches up to ten or twelve feet from the ground. As the seasons passed, I began to notice a violet here and there, and a strawberry-like ground cover with a pretty yellow flower; but these things couldn't be appreciated because they were sparse and overgrown. I was shocked to find that there wasn't a fern on the place anywhere, not a daisy, not even a buttercup. No black-eyed Susans, no Queen Anne's lace. I might not know anything about gardening, but I knew that a house in the country ought to have at least these basic field flowers. I cast my mind back to the wooded hillsides of my childhood and recalled jack-in-the-pulpit and bunchflower and trailing arbutus and lady's-slipper.

Then I thought about this place as a real home, probably destined to become our retirement home and until then a place where the children could come for vacations. While we all liked the idea of a 'wild place', maybe it could be tamed just a little so as to have some touches of brightness and colour to mark the progress of the seasons. How about a lilac? Lilac is the very essence of home. I'd never thought about it before, but I did now. A home *should* have a lilac bush – it's just something a *home should have*.

I was determined to keep it a wild place, but the more I thought about it, the more my imagination conjured up a *beautiful* wild place, an ideal wild place, a twice-as-good-as-nature wild place. I began to read books about shady gardens and 'natural' gardens and – looking at the glacial deposits of granite liberally strewn around – rock gardens. And I began, perforce, to learn the elements of gardening.

It's a fascinating subject, like all subjects when they are tackled seriously. I read everything and I tried – almost everything. The compost pile I had of course started immediately, with the brush cleared to open up paths. I learned about, and tried, raising plants from seed (both wild and cultivated); transplanting as it should properly be done; soil preparation and improvement; layering and other methods of propagation; pruning; garden layout and home landscaping in general. (It was a little late for that, but you have to start from where you are.)

Little by little my ideas crystallised and I began to put them into practice. More often than not they failed, and then I would try to figure out whether this was because I hadn't done it right or because there was some reason why this particular idea was not workable for that particular space.

Often it was the latter; and more and more I came to the philosophical view that the most convincing results of 'natural' gardening were to be achieved by *letting* things happen and *encouraging* them to happen rather than *forcing* them to happen.

By the second summer I was a confirmed worker-on-the-land. On weekends, and for a month in the summer, I would get up at dawn and work for anywhere from five to twelve hours; and this intense level of activity continued for a number of years. That a high proportion of these efforts came to naught in the way of fulfillment of my original ideas I have never resented. I have come to realise that in gardening, as in fishing, the manifest results are the least important benefits of the activity. Just being there is what is important – 'simply messing about' in your garden, smelling the good earth, pouring out what our family calls mother juice (it was good to have another outlet for my nurturant nature, my children being now well along in adolescence). What is important is the dreaming and the planning, and the seeing it in one's mind's eye, so much more glorious than it ever is in reality.

One never sees one's garden as it is *this* year. There are occasional small triumphs, but the overall effect is never quite what you had in mind – or if it is, you have a new idea in mind by now. Those campanulas look too spotty, they should be grouped closer together. Wouldn't a bit of pink be good at the end of this arrangement? That lovely, dark mysterious corner would be even more satisfying with a small silvery-white something in its depths, reflecting the light and pointing up the darkness. Let's get rid of that intrusive branch at the corner of the path; it distracts your attention just when you should be focusing on the expanding woodland vista.

A person who is preoccupied with such imaginings and

spends significant amounts of time trying to bring them to realisation must, I think, be considered a gardener, and from this period I so considered myself. Against all expectation and all intention the metamorphosis had occurred.

From **My Garden and I,** *published by Lyons and Burford Publishers.*

CONTRIBUTORS' NOTES

Bridget and Maureen Boland are not old wives but spinsters and sisters.

Bridget Boland is well known as a playwright (*The Prisoner*), screenwriter (*Gaslight, Anne of the Thousand Days*), and novelist. Maureen Boland joined London's BT Batsford bookshop in 1931 and worked there for 27 years. In 1964 she became head of the art books department of Hatchards in Piccadilly, where she worked until shortly before her death in September 1976.

The two sisters were always great gardeners – first in London, where their 20 × 20 foot back garden was opened by request to the public, and was much photographed for books and magazines; and for some years in Hampshire. Their move gave rise to an urgent need for advice, as the methods they had used in London were of little use in the country. They pestered everyone they met for help, and so began the accumulation of gardening lore from which *The Complete Old Wives' Lore for Gardens* was compiled.

Jean Buffong is a Grenadian novelist who has lived in England since 1962. Her novella, *Jump-Up-and-Kiss-Me*, was published by The Women's Press in 1990, and was followed by the novels *Under the Silk Cotton Tree* (The Women's Press, 1992) and *Snowflakes in the Sun* (The Women's Press, 1994).

Sidonie Gabrielle Colette was born in Burgundy in 1873 and died in Paris in 1954. She began to write under the tutelage of her first husband, 'Willy', under whose name her famous Claudine novels were originally published. In 1906, Colette embarked on a second career on the music hall stage, where she became associated with the Paris *demi-monde* of Natalie Clifford Barney and Renee Vivien. She wrote for *Le Matin* and continued writing throughout her long life. Autobiographical themes – her mother, Provence, animals and nature – reverberate throughout her novels and prose. Colette's words include *Gigi, Chéri, The Vagabond, My Mother's House, Duo and Le Toutounier, Break of Day, Looking Backwards* and *The Evening Star: Recollections*.

Margaret Fuller was born in 1936 and has been gardening since she could walk. She has lived at The Crossing House for 37 years – and her garden at the house is open to the public every day of the year.

Germaine Greer's first book *The Female Eunuch* (1969), was an international bestseller. Her subsequent books include *The Obstacle Race, Sex and Destiny, The Madwoman's Underclothes, Kissing the Rod* (ed.), *Daddy, We Hardly Knew You, The Change* and *Slip-Shod Sibyls*. She now teaches at Newnham College, Cambridge.

Kiran Grewal is a fine arts graduate currently working on writing short stories and tending to her window-box garden of marguerites, miniature roses and forget-me-nots, which help to heal and soothe her troubled urban soul. Her work has been published in *Pulp Fiction* and she is a member of the Asian Women Writers' Collective.

Clare Hastings is a costume designer and the daughter of the gardening writer Anne Scott-James. After an untroubled childhood free from thoughts of ground frost and greenfly, she gave in to the family genes at the age of 40, and is now slave to a cottage garden in Berkshire and a roof in London.

Susan Hill was born in Scarborough, Yorkshire in 1942. Her novels include *Gentleman and Ladies*, *A Change for the Better*, *I'm the King of the Castle* (Somerset Maugham Award), *The Albatross and Other Stories* (John Llewellyn Rhys Prize), *Strange Meeting*, *The Bird of Night* (Whitbread Prize), *In the Spring-time of the Year* and *The Woman in Black*. She has also written two autobiographical books, *The Magic Apple Tree*, as well as topographical books and for children. She is a regular broadcaster and reviewer. Susan Hill is married to the Shakespeare scholar Stanley Wells. They have two daughters and live in Gloucestershire.

Gertrude Jekyll was born in 1843 and enjoyed a considerable reputation as an artist and craftswoman before becoming a gardener. During her lifetime she was acknowledged as one of the great authorities on English gardens and gardening. She revolutionised garden thinking, created many beautiful gardens herself and must be given much of the credit for introducing the herbaceous border – so quintessential a part of the English garden. Using her sympathetic understanding of colour, which she developed as an artist, to obtain in plants superb juxtapositioning of both textures and colours, she became thought of as a flower artist. Since her death in 1932, Gertrude Jekyll's thoughts and philosophies have endured and her creative ideas and practical advice are still valued and followed by gardeners and designers today.

Manju Kak has been a teacher of history, a broadcaster, painter, writer and compère. She is the author of *First Light in Coonelpura* and *Requiem for an Unsung Revolutionary*. Her articles, reviews and features have been published in various newspapers, journals and magazines; and she has won awards for her short stories which have appeared in various anthologies including *In Other Words: New Writing by Indian Women* (The Women's Press, 1993). Manju Kak divides her time between New Delhi and the Kumaon Hills in the Himalayas where she schooled.

Gretchen Legler was born and raised in Salt Lake City, Utah. She has worked as an agricultural journalist and feature writer for newspapers in Minnesota and North Dakota. She has a Master's Degree in creative writing from the University of Minnesota, where she is also completing a Ph.D. dissertation on women nature writers. Her short stories and essays have appeared in the *Indiana Review, Grain, Hurricane Alice, The House on Via Gombito: Writing by North American Women Abroad, Uncommon Waters: Women Write About Fishing*, and *A Different Angle: Fly Fishing Stories by Women*. Her collection of essays, *All the Powerful Invisible Things*, is her first book-length work.

Clare Leighton was born in 1898 and died in 1989. *Four Hedges: A Gardener's Chronicle* was written and engraved in 1935, during what was perhaps the happiest period in her life. She had achieved early recognition as a gifted wood-engraver, and as the daughter of two writers, felt called to convey in words as well as wood her delight in gardening as a souce of contentment and wisdom. In 1939, Clare Leighton emigrated from Britain to the United States, where her accurate and sympathetic recording in words and images of life on the land helped her to 'grow new roots' for herself. In later years, she turned to designing stained glass windows and mosaics, but never lost her wonder at the miracle of seed-time, flowering and harvest.

Mary Russell Mitford (1787–1855) was born of a father whose extravagance and gambling compelled her to try to earn a living as a writer. She published a volume of verse in 1810, and was encouraged to continue writing by Coleridge. Further volumes of poems appeared, and various essays in magazines, then in 1823 her drama *Julian* was produced successfully at Covent Garden, and was followed by the even more successful *Foscari* in 1826 and *Rienzi* in 1828. She wrote other historical dramas, but meanwhile, in 1824, she had begun a series of sketches and stories which made up *Our Village* (1832), the work by which she is remembered. This was followed by *Belford Regis* (1835), a portrait of Reading; *Country Stories* (1837); and *Recollections of a Literary Life* (1852); a novel, *Atherton, and other Tales*, was published in 1854. Her letters to Lamb, Haydon, Horne, Ruskin, Elizabeth Barrett Browning, W S Landor and many others have also been widely published.

Drusilla Modjeska was born in Britain in 1946 and has lived in Australia since 1971. She is the author of *Exiles at Home*, *Poppy* and *The Orchard* (The Women's Press, 1997) winner of the Australian Booksellers Award, the NSW Premier's Award and the Kibble Literary Prize.

Mirabel Osler writes regularly for the gardening quarterly *Hortus*, and for a range of other British and American periodicals. Her first book, *A Gentle Plea for Chaos* was published in 1989 and since then she has written two more garden books and a book about the legendary food of France. She lives in the Shropshire town of Ludlow.

Jill Parker, married to Sir Peter Parker and with four grown children spent all her working life as a GP in a National Health practice in London. In the 1970s, the Parkers bought a medieval Cotswold farmhouse with five acres of derelict garden. Since then, Jill Parker has been creating a romantic garden with old roses, rambling shrubs and borders around the old trees which 'will never be finished, thank goodness'.

Eleanor Perényi was born in Washington DC, the daughter of an American naval officer and a novelist. She was brought up in Europe, China, the Caribbean, and various parts of the United States – wherever her father was stationed. At 19 she married Baron Zsigmond Perényi and lived on his estate in Hungary for many years. She worked on various magazines in New York City, including *Mademoiselle*. The author of *Liszt: The Artist as Romantic Hero*, she has written for the *Atlantic Monthly*, *Harper's*, *Esquire* and *Harper's Bazaar*. She has one son, who is in the US Foreign Service. Her garden is in Stonington, Connecticut, where she has lived for more than 30 years.

Olive Pitkin lived in New York City before buying her country house in Watch Hill, Rhode Island. She continues to split her time between the two, along with her husband.

Miriam Rothschild was born in 1908 and has worked as a marine biologist amongst much else. In 1970, she moved into the family home at Ashton Wold and began to cultivate wild flowers. She developed her 'farmer's nightmare' seed mixture of cornflowers, corn marigold, corncockle, poppies and mayweed – plants that farmers had tried to eradicate for centuries – and is now an acknowledged expert on the preservation and re-introduction of Britain's native flora. Her commissions include the planting of swards at Stansted Airport, and she is known for her book, *The Butterfly Gardener*, and her television programme with Ladybird Johnson about roadside verges in Britain and Texas. A member of the executive committee of the Society for the Promotion of Nature Reserves for over 30 years, she has been awarded the Victoria Medal of Honour.

May Sarton is an internationally acclaimed diarist, novelist and poet. Her much-loved series of autobiographical works published by The Women's Press include her bestselling *Journal of a Solitude* (1985), *After the Stroke* (1988), *Endgame* (1992), *Encore* (1993), *I Knew a Phoenix* (1995), *The House by the Sea* (1995), *A World of Light* (1996), *At Eighty-two* (1996) and *Plant Dreaming Deep* (1996).

The Women's Press also publish May Sarton's novels, including her classic early work, *Mrs Stevens Hears the Mermaids Singing* (1993), the first in which she wrote openly of homosexual love, *As We Are Now* (1993), *A Reckoning* (1984), *The Magnificent Spinster* (1986), *The Education of Harriet Hatfield* (1990), *Kinds of Love* (1995), *A Shower of Summer Days* (1995), *The Single Hound* (1996) and *The Small Room* (1996). Her specially selected volumes of poetry, *Halfway to Silence* and *Coming into Eighty and Earlier Poems*, were published by The Women's Press in 1993 and 1995 respectively. May Sarton is also the author of *Writings on Writing*, a collection of essays about her craft and art (The Women's Press, 1995).

May Sarton was born in Europe, but for most of her life made the East Coast of America her home. She died in July 1995, aged 83, in York, Maine.

Emily Eldridge Saville grew up on the East Coast of America. Her memories of her childhood were self-published as *Memories and a Garden* in 1924.

Alice B Toklas was born in San Francisco in 1877 where she lived until leaving for Paris with journalist Harriet Levy in 1907. There she met and fell in love with Gertrude Stein, moving in with her in 1910. The couple were inseparable until Stein's death in 1946, and Alice B Toklas celebrated their life together in *The Alice B Toklas Cookbook*, first published in 1954. Her other books include *Aromas and Flavors of Past and Present* and *What is Remembered*.

Latha Viswanathan is a freelance writer and editor living in Baton Rouge, Louisiana. She has worked as a journalist and advertising copywriter in India, England and Canada. Her short fiction has appeared in numerous American literary journals. In 1994, she won the John Hazard Wildman Prize for fiction given by Louisiana State University.

Alice Walker was born in Eatonton, Georgia. She has received many awards, including The Radcliffe Fellowship and a Guggenheim Fellowship. Her hugely popular novel, *The Color Purple* (The Women's Press, 1983), won the American Book Award, plus the Pulitzer Prize for Fiction in 1983, and was subsequently made into an internationally successful film by Steven Spielberg.

Alice Walker's other novels are *Meridian* (The Women's Press, 1982), of which CLR James said, 'I have not read a novel superior to this'; *The Third Life of Grange Copeland* (The Women's Press, 1985); *The Temple of My Familiar* (The Women's Press, 1989), which appeared in the *New York Times* bestseller list for four months; and *Possessing the Secret of Joy*

(1992). She has written two collections of short stories: *In Love and Trouble* (The Women's Press, 1984), and *You Can't Keep a Good Woman Down* (The Women's Press, 1982); and two books of essays and memoirs: *In Search of Our Mothers' Gardens: Womanist Prose* (The Women's Press, 1984), and *Living by the Word* (The Women's Press, 1988). Alice Walker has published four books of poetry, all of which have been published by The Women's Press: *Horses Make a Landscape Look More Beautiful* (1985), *Once* (1986), *Good Night, Willie Lee, I'll See You in the Morning* (1987) and *Revolutionary Petunias* (1988).

Alice Walker's complete poetry is now collected together in *Her Blue Body Everything We Know: Earthling Poems 1965–1990 Complete* (1991) and her complete short stories appear in *The Complete Stories* (1994), both published by The Women's Press. Her full-length work of autobiography *The Same River Twice: Honoring the Difficult*, was published by The Women's Press in 1996.

Louise Beebe Wilder (1878–1938) was an influential figure in American gardening between the two world wars. In her classic book, *Color in the Garden* (1918), based on the year-round seasons at Balderbrae, her summer home near Pomona, New York, she led a new generation of gardeners away from the then prevailing style of 'English gardening' by the simple use of good designs and first rate plantswomanship.

The Women's Press is Britain's leading women's publishing house. Established in 1978, we publish high-quality fiction and non-fiction from outstanding women writers worldwide. Our exciting and diverse list includes literary fiction, detective novels, biography and autobiography, health, women's studies, handbooks, literary criticism, psychology and self help, the arts, our popular Livewire Books series for young women and the bestselling annual *Women Artists Diary* featuring beautiful colour and black-and-white illustrations from the best in contemporary women's art.

If you would like more information about our books or about our mail order book club, please send an A5 sae for our latest catalogue and complete list to:

The Sales Department
The Women's Press Ltd
34 Great Sutton Street
London EC1V 0DX
Tel: 0171 251 3007
Fax: 0171 608 1938